WILLIAMS-SONOMA

NEW FLAVORS FOR
vegetables

RECIPES
Jodi Liano

PHOTOGRAPHS
Kate Sears

Oxmoor
House®

spring

summer

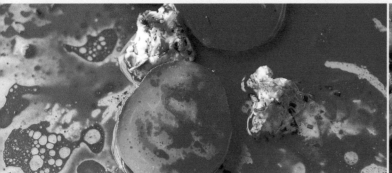

fall

winter

introducing new flavors

"Eat your vegetables!" We've all heard it. In fact, we've probably all said it. Vegetables have always been an essential part of our diets, but they've often been somewhat of an afterthought—just boiled, roasted, or steamed to accompany the main dish. Today, with weekly farmers' markets in many cities, grocery stores stocking more varied produce, and an international pantry of exciting flavors to choose from, what used to be the bit player of any complete dinner menu has evolved into the meal's rising star.

The forty-four recipes in this book are inspired by familiar side dishes and seasonal produce, but offer a twist by introducing a variety of unexpected flavor pairings. Basic ingredients are cooked in ways that intensify their impact: butter is cooked until lightly browned and nutty; onions are braised in broth until tender and rich. Condiments from around the world, such as sweet white miso paste and Moroccan harissa, add bursts of flavor to give unique character to once forgettable side dishes.

This book is organized according to the seasons to give you an idea of when certain vegetables will be at the height of their ripeness. Cooking methods are often influenced by the seasons too: outdoor grilling is enticing on a warm summer evening, while the intense flavors of roasting are more inviting during the cold months. That said, many of these dishes can be made throughout the year, so just flip through the book and select what sounds best. With a variety of flavors to choose from, we hope you'll find a handful of dishes to add to your repertoire.

freshness as an ingredient

When food is fresh, the simple addition of a few bright flavors will have you savoring every last bite. Think of freshness as the most important ingredient and your vegetable dishes will only get better from there.

seasonal Whether it's spring peas in their pods fragrant and sweet; fresh August corn plucked from the stalk that morning; or creamy, rich butternut squash in the late fall, nothing beats the flavor of vegetables picked and prepared at their peak. You don't have to memorize what's in season in your area to buy vegetables at their freshest, just keep a few things in mind: Vegetables should feel heavy for their size, have leaves that are unblemished, and skins that are tight and smooth. For some vegetables, smell tells you everything. Tomatoes, for example, should smell sweet and like the vine from which they were picked.

local An easy way to ensure that what you're buying is fresh is to visit your neighborhood farmers' market, where what's for sale could have been plucked from the ground that same day. When it comes to taste, there's really no substitute for buying farm-fresh ingredients like this. More and more, you can also find local produce on sale at grocery stores and natural-foods stores.

organic Whenever possible, try to buy organic vegetables, which haven't been grown or treated with chemicals and often taste better than the conventional varieties. Organic vegetables also have a shorter shelf life, so when you see them in the store, they are often at the height of their ripeness.

being bold

Adding just a few unexpected flavor twists to everyday vegetable preparations takes them to a whole new level. Bold sauces and pastes; fragrant, fresh herbs; and earthy toasted spices used in combination with smart techniques will create delicious, memorable vegetable accompaniments or even standalone meals.

global flavors Harissa. Wasabi. Sriracha sauce. Miso. Take a peek inside your pantry—these condiments may be missing. These seasonings are worth seeking out in the ethnic aisle of your grocery store or specialty-food store, though, because just a small amount can transform a simple vegetable dish. In these recipes, we use just a dollop of wasabi to add a hint of heat to simple mashed potatoes; or a couple teaspoons of Indian curry powder to give new life to roasted root vegetables.

high-impact cooking methods Caramelizing and braising, cooking methods often used with meats, can add similar depth of flavor to vegetables. Cauliflower becomes crisp and sweet when roasted at a high heat until caramelized. Braising hearty winter greens in a spiced broth creates a satisfying dish that pairs perfectly with roasted meats in the winter. Don't underestimate the power of your grill, either; it imparts a smokiness to fresh vegetables that can't be matched.

unexpected pairings In these pages, classic dishes are reinvented with just a few new flavors. For example, a fresh take on the crudité platter pairs blanched green beans with a tangy crème fraîche–tarragon dipping sauce; pesto with arugula and walnuts makes a peppery sauce for sauteed tomatoes.

flavors in layers

Successful vegetable dishes are simple and satisfying, yet still play with a variety of flavors, textures, and temperatures. Tasting and seasoning throughout the cooking process also helps ensure that every bite is packed with flavor.

seasoning with salt In these recipes, you will see salt, mostly sea salt, added several times during cooking; this is to bring out the distinct flavors of each ingredient and also to tie the flavors together. In some recipes, other ingredients, like Thai fish sauce, preserved anchovies, or Parmesan cheese, stand in for the salt.

complement and contrast Layering similar or contrasting flavors throughout a dish can make it uniquely delicious. These recipes use citrus juice and zest often to draw out the natural flavors of vegetables; fresh herbs are used to brighten earthy fall and winter vegetables; and sauces are made with surprising ingredient combinations like chiles and honey, or harissa and minted yogurt.

texture and temperature Using ingredients with opposing textures and temperatures is another way to add new twists to familiar vegetable dishes. In these recipes, radicchio is grilled until sweet and smoky, then topped with a room-temperature, pungent salsa verde; and a crunchy bread-crumb mixture is stuffed between the leaves of an artichoke to complement its tender flesh.

As you flip through these pages, step a bit out of your comfort zone and try some new things. You might just be surprised what these new flavors can do to your old favorites. "Eat your vegetables" will take on a whole new meaning.

spring

snow pea and radish salad

snow peas, ½ pound

radishes, 5

rice vinegar,
1½ tablespoons

honey, ½ teaspoon

sea salt and freshly
ground pepper

canola oil, ¼ cup

fresh mint, leaves from
2 sprigs, cut into thin
ribbons

MAKES 4 SERVINGS

Bring a large pot of salted water to a boil over high heat. Fill a large bowl two-thirds full with ice water.

Remove the strings from the snow peas. Add the snow peas to the boiling water and cook for 1½ minutes. Drain the peas and then immediately plunge them into the ice water. Let stand for a minute or two, then drain the snow peas and pat dry.

Cut the snow peas on the diagonal into 1-inch pieces and place in a bowl. Thinly slice the radishes, then cut the slices into thin strips. Add the radishes to the bowl with the snow peas.

In a small bowl, whisk together the vinegar, honey, and a pinch each of salt and pepper. Add the oil in a slow, steady stream and whisk to blend. Taste and adjust the seasonings.

Add enough dressing to coat the snow peas and radishes and toss well to coat; you may not need it all. Add the mint to the salad and toss gently to mix. Serve right away.

Cutting the radishes into thin slivers tempers their peppery bite and spreads it evenly throughout the dish. The sweet-tart honey-vinegar dressing provides a contrast to the spicy radishes and plays along with the sweetness of the snow peas in this springtime salad.

sweet and sour **vidalia onions**

Vidalia onions are full of natural sugars which soften their pungency. Slow-cooking them in a bath of sugar-fortified red-wine vinegar and chicken broth accentuates the inherent sweetness of the vegetable. This cooking liquid doubles as a rich, butter-free sauce, accented by mellow roasted garlic and woodsy fresh thyme.

Preheat the oven to 350°F.

Peel and quarter the onions, leaving just enough of the root end attached to keep the wedges together. Arrange the onions in a roasting pan in a single layer and sprinkle lightly with salt and pepper. On a cutting board with the side of a large knife, mash the garlic clove and add it to the dish, then add the thyme sprigs and bay leaf. Drizzle the oil over the onions.

In a small saucepan over medium-high heat, bring the 1 cup broth to a boil. Add the vinegar and sugar and cook, stirring occasionally, until the sugar has dissolved, 2–3 minutes.

Pour the broth mixture over the onions. There should be enough to come halfway up the sides of the onions. Add a bit more chicken broth, if needed. Cover the dish tightly with aluminum foil.

Bake the onions, stirring occasionally, until they release some of their juice and begin to soften, 30–40 minutes. Carefully remove the foil, raise the oven temperature to 400°F, and bake, stirring occasionally, until the liquid has reduced to about 2 tablespoons and the onions are very soft, 60–75 minutes longer.

Transfer the onions to a serving dish and serve hot or at room temperature.

vidalia onions, 4

sea salt and freshly ground pepper

garlic, 1 clove

fresh thyme, 3 sprigs

dried bay leaf, 1

extra-virgin olive oil, 1 tablespoon

low-sodium chicken broth, 1 cup, plus broth as needed

cabernet wine vinegar, 3 tablespoons

sugar, 2 tablespoons

MAKES 4 SERVINGS

The unique flavor of fava beans, a quintessential springtime vegetable, is nicely highlighted by marjoram, the mild, floral-scented cousin of oregano. The herb's minty, citrusy hints blend into the background to let the fava beans shine.

fava bean sauté with marjoram and feta

This recipe celebrates the spring fava bean harvest by using ingredients that enhance but do not mask the fresh, nutty flavor and buttery texture of the legume. Feta cheese adds a bright tanginess; both shallot and lemon zest contribute a pleasing zip; and marjoram's mellow, floral hints bring all the elements together.

Bring a large pot of salted water to a boil. Fill a large bowl two-thirds full with ice water. Remove the fava beans from the pods; discard the pods.

Add the beans to the boiling water and cook for 2 minutes. Drain the beans and then immediately plunge them into the ice water. When the beans are cool enough to handle, slip off the tough outer skins by pinching one end of the beans. Place the shelled beans in a bowl and pat dry.

In a frying pan over medium heat, warm the oil. When the oil is hot, add the shallot and a pinch of salt and sauté until the shallot is soft and translucent, 3–4 minutes. Add the fava beans and another pinch of salt and sauté for 2 minutes. Add the marjoram and sauté until the beans are just tender, 1–2 minutes longer.

Remove the pan from the heat. Squeeze the juice from the lemon half over the beans and stir to mix. Taste and adjust the seasonings with salt and pepper. Transfer the beans to a warmed serving dish and crumble the cheese over the top. Serve right away.

fava beans in the pods, 2 pounds

extra-virgin olive oil, 1 tablespoon

shallot, ¼, thinly sliced

sea salt and freshly ground pepper

fresh marjoram, 2 teaspoons minced

lemon, ½

feta cheese, 1 ounce

MAKES 4 SERVINGS

marinated grilled baby leeks

baby leeks, 16

sherry vinegar,
2 tablespoons

dijon mustard, 1 teaspoon

**sea salt and freshly
ground pepper**

chives, 1½ tablespoons
minced

**fresh chervil or flat-leaf
parsley,** 1 tablespoon
minced, plus whole leaves
for sprinkling

**peppery extra-virgin
olive oil,** ½ cup

MAKES 4 SERVINGS

Trim the root ends from the leeks, leaving just enough attached to keep the leeks from falling apart.

In a rectangular glass baking dish, combine the vinegar, mustard, a pinch each of salt and pepper, 1 tablespoon of the chives, and the 1 tablespoon minced chervil. Whisk together until well blended. Add the oil in a slow, steady stream and whisk to blend. Place the leeks in the dish and toss to coat them well. Cover the dish with plastic wrap and marinate the leeks at room temperature for at least 1 hour or refrigerate for up to overnight.

Ten to twenty minutes before you plan to serve the leeks, prepare a charcoal or gas grill for direct-heat grilling over medium-high heat. Remove the leeks from the marinade, shaking off any excess, and reserve the marinade. Arrange the leeks on the grill rack and cook until tender and nicely browned, 5–6 minutes, turning occasionally to cook the leeks evenly.

Transfer the leeks to a warmed platter and drizzle lightly with some of the remaining marinade. Sprinkle with the remaining chives and the chervil leaves. Serve hot or at room temperature.

Anise-scented chervil contributes its unique herbaceousness to this dish of smoke-tinged baby leeks. The sweet young alliums are accented by nutty sherry vinegar, pungent Dijon mustard, and peppery olive oil, a mixture that doubles as both marinade and sauce.

Serving artichokes whole lets diners enjoy the sensual act of peeling away the leaves one by one to enjoy the tender flesh. Stuffing the cavities with a mixture of olive-oil coated bread crumbs, spicy red pepper flakes, and cooling fresh mint alleviates the need for a sauce.

stuffed roasted artichokes with chile and mint

lemon, 1

globe artichokes, 4

unsalted butter,
1 tablespoon

extra-virgin olive oil,
1 tablespoon, plus oil
for drizzling

yellow onion, 1, finely
diced

sea salt and freshly
ground pepper

jalapeño chile, 1, seeded
and minced

garlic, 2 cloves, minced

red pepper flakes,
½ teaspoon

fresh bread crumbs
(page 145), 1½ cups

large egg, 1

fresh mint, leaves from
½ bunch, cut into thin
ribbons

MAKES 4 SERVINGS

Bring a large pot of salted water to a boil. Halve the lemon, squeeze the juice into the boiling water, and carefully drop in the lemon halves. Using a sharp knife, cut off the top fourth of each artichoke, then trim the stem flush with the bottom. Using kitchen shears, cut the sharp tips off the leaves. Lower the artichokes into the boiling water and cook, turning occasionally, until the bottoms are almost tender when pierced with a knife and the leaves come off when pulled firmly, 15–20 minutes. Drain the artichokes upside down on a rack set over a baking sheet.

In a saucepan over medium heat, melt the butter with the 1 tablespoon oil. Add the onion and a pinch of salt and sauté until the onion is soft and translucent, 5–6 minutes. Add the chile, garlic, and red pepper flakes and sauté for 2 minutes. Turn off the heat, stir in the bread crumbs, and transfer the mixture to a bowl. Add the egg and beat well with a fork until the mixture is well moistened. Add the mint to the mixture along with a generous pinch each of salt and pepper and stir to blend.

Preheat the oven to 350°F. When cool enough to handle, gently open the artichoke leaves away from the center and remove the tough chokes and small yellow leaves using a sturdy spoon. Fill the cavity of each artichoke and the spaces between some of the leaves with the crumb mixture. Arrange the artichokes snugly in a baking dish and drizzle the tops with oil. Cover with aluminum foil and bake until the leaves pull out easily, about 20 minutes. Remove the foil and bake until the top of the filling is lightly browned, about 10 minutes longer.

Transfer the artichokes to warmed plates and serve right away.

The earthy, nutty flavor of artichokes, as well as their unique shape, with many natural pockets to fill, make them great vehicles for bold seasonings like the garlic and two types of chile in this stuffing. The refreshing quality of mint counteracts the spice from the jalapeño and the richness of the oil-coated bread crumbs.

Choose the highest quality eggs you can find, cook them lightly, and their bright-orange yolks and creamy texture will stand in for sauce to guild fresh asparagus spears. Here, the vegetable is roasted at a high temperature to bring out a natural nuttiness, which is echoed by the grated Parmesan that is sprinkled over the top.

Keto

roasted asparagus with fried eggs and parmesan

Preheat the oven to 425°F.

Break off the tough end of each asparagus spear about 1 inch from the base. (If the spears are thick, use a vegetable peeler to remove the peel from the bottom half.) Place the spears on a baking sheet, drizzle with the oil, and toss well to coat. Sprinkle lightly with salt and pepper. Roast until the spears are just tender when pierced with a small knife, 10–12 minutes.

While the asparagus is roasting, melt 1 tablespoon of the butter in a large nonstick frying pan over medium-low heat. Break 2 of the eggs into the pan, spacing them a couple of inches apart so they do not touch. Cover the pan and cook the eggs for 2 minutes. Uncover and cook until the whites are opaque and the yolks are still runny, 2–3 minutes.

Divide the asparagus among 4 warmed plates. Using a slotted spatula, carefully lift each egg and place it next to but slightly overlapping a serving of asparagus. Sprinkle the eggs lightly with salt and pepper. Immediately grate some of the Parmesan cheese over the dish. Repeat with the remaining 2 eggs and serve right away.

asparagus spears,
1½ pounds

extra-virgin olive oil,
2 tablespoons

sea salt and freshly ground pepper

unsalted butter,
2 tablespoons

large eggs, 4

parmesan cheese,
small chunk

MAKES 4 SERVINGS

sautéed english peas with garlic and sesame

sesame seeds,
2 tablespoons

english peas, 3 pounds,
shelled

extra-virgin olive oil,
1 tablespoon

asian sesame oil,
1 teaspoon

garlic, 2 cloves, minced

**sea salt and freshly
ground pepper**

MAKES 4 SERVINGS

In a dry pan over medium heat, toast the sesame seeds until golden brown and fragrant, 4–5 minutes. Pour onto a plate and set aside to cool.

Bring a large pot of salted water to a boil. Fill a large bowl two-thirds full with ice water. Add the peas to the boiling water and cook for 2–3 minutes. Drain the peas and then immediately plunge them into the ice water. Let stand for a minute or two, then drain.

In a large frying pan over medium-high heat, warm the olive and sesame oils. When the oils are hot, add the garlic and sauté, stirring constantly, until it is fragrant but not brown, about 30 seconds.

Add the peas and a pinch each of salt and pepper, and sauté, tossing and stirring occasionally, until the peas are just tender, 3–4 minutes. Sprinkle with the toasted sesame seeds and stir well. Taste and adjust the seasonings. Serve right away.

A sprinkling of toasted sesame seeds adds a layer of nuttiness along with some crunch to bright, fresh-from-the-garden peas. Silky sesame oil provides another layer of earthiness, while the garlic contributes a pungent counterpoint.

Infusing olive oil with chives makes a vibrantly-colored condiment with an onion-like taste. Drizzled over steamed new potatoes, with their thin skins and mildly earthy flavor, the oil becomes a silky alternative to the usual coating of butter.

steamed new potatoes with chive oil

small new potatoes such as fingerling, Yukon gold, or baby red, 2 pounds, each about 1½ inches in diameter

fresh chives, 1 bunch

fruity extra-virgin olive oil, ⅓ cup

lemon, 1

sea salt and freshly ground pepper

MAKES 4 SERVINGS

Scrub the potatoes and, if necessary, halve any large ones so they are all about the same size. Bring 1–2 inches of water to a boil in a saucepan and place the potatoes in a steamer rack that just fits the pot. Steam the potatoes, covered, until a sharp knife penetrates the potatoes easily, with no resistance, 15–17 minutes.

While the potatoes are cooking, bring a small saucepan of water to a boil. Fill a small bowl two-thirds full with ice water. Coarsely chop three-fourths of the chives. Add them to the boiling water and cook for 1 minute. Drain the chives and then immediately plunge them into the ice water. Let stand for a minute or two, then drain and pat dry. Place the chives in a blender or mini food processor. With the motor running, pour in the olive oil and blend until smooth. Pass the chive oil through a fine-mesh strainer lined with a paper towel into a small bowl. Discard the chives that cling to the paper towel along with the paper towel.

Cut the remaining chives into 1-inch pieces. Finely grate the zest from the lemon (reserve the fruit for another use). When the potatoes are done, place them in a warmed serving dish. Add the chive pieces and chive oil and toss gently to mix. Taste and adjust the seasonings with salt and pepper. Sprinkle with the lemon zest and serve right away.

For this recipe, using a fruity olive oil (as opposed to a peppery one) to blend with the chives helps balance the oniony flavor in the bold-tasting, vibrant green drizzling oil. The infused oil forms an innovative sauce for simply steamed new potatoes, which are accented by the brightness of lemon zest.

sautéed baby spinach with lemon zest and cream

The zest of citrus contains the fruit's essential oil and is packed with bold flavor. Used first in strips to infuse into the cream sauce, then finely grated and mixed with the cooked spinach, the layers of lemon brighten this otherwise rich, creamy dish with their vibrance.

Pour the cream into a saucepan. Using a vegetable peeler, peel 2 strips of lemon zest, each 2 inches long, from the lemon. Set the lemon aside. Add the zest strips to the cream and bring to a simmer over medium heat. Cook the cream, stirring occasionally, until reduced by half, about 8 minutes; watch that the cream does not boil too vigorously. Remove the zest strips and discard.

Remove any tough stems from the spinach leaves and rinse them well in a colander. Heat a large frying pan over medium heat. Add the spinach, with the rinsing water still clinging to the leaves. Sprinkle with the sugar and toss well. Cover the pan and cook the spinach for 3 minutes. Uncover and toss the leaves well. Continue to cook, uncovered, until the spinach is wilted and tender, 1–2 minutes.

Place the spinach in a colander and, using a wooden spoon, press on it firmly to remove all the excess liquid. Chop the drained spinach coarsely and add it to the pan with the reduced cream. Finely grate the remaining lemon zest and add to the spinach (reserve the fruit for another use). Season the spinach with a pinch of salt and about ½ teaspoon pepper and stir well to combine. Cook over medium heat, stirring occasionally, until just heated through, 2–3 minutes.

Transfer the spinach to a warmed serving bowl and serve right away.

heavy cream, 1 cup

lemon, 1

baby spinach, 2 pounds

sugar, 1 teaspoon

sea salt and freshly ground pepper

MAKES 4 SERVINGS

artichoke ragout with garlic, saffron, and orange zest

lemon, 1

globe artichokes, 6

orange, 1

extra-virgin olive oil,
2 tablespoons

yellow onion, 1/2, finely
diced

sea salt and freshly
ground pepper

garlic, 2 cloves, minced

dry white wine such as
sauvignon blanc, 1 cup

saffron threads, 6–8

MAKES 4 SERVINGS

Fill a large bowl with cold water. Halve the lemon, squeeze the juice into the water, and drop in the lemon halves. Pull off and discard the tough outer leaves from each artichoke. Using a sharp knife, cut off the top of the artichoke about 1 inch above the base, or heart. Using a paring knife, trim off the dark green flesh from the base and stem of the artichoke. Cut the artichoke in half and scoop out the fuzzy chokes with a sturdy spoon. Cut the halves into 1-inch wedges and place in the bowl of lemon water.

Finely grate the zest from the orange and then squeeze the juice to measure about 1/2 cup. Set the zest and juice aside.

In a sauté pan over medium-low heat, warm the oil. When the oil is hot, add the onion and a pinch of salt and sauté until the onion is soft and translucent, 6–7 minutes. Add the garlic and sauté for 1 minute longer. Drain the artichokes and add them to the pan along with the orange juice, wine, and 1/2 cup water. Crumble the saffron threads and sprinkle them into the pan. Bring the mixture to a boil, then reduce the heat to low. Add a generous pinch each of salt and pepper, cover the pan, and simmer until the artichokes are just tender when pierced with a knife, about 25 minutes.

Uncover the pan, increase the heat to medium-high, and simmer vigorously until the liquid reduces to a glaze, 6–7 minutes. Add half of the reserved orange zest and stir to mix. Taste and adjust the seasonings.

Transfer the artichokes to a warmed serving dish and sprinkle with the remaining orange zest. Serve hot or at room temperature.

Artichokes absorb flavor from marinades and sauces especially well. In this recipe, the vegetable cooks in a broth of fragrant saffron, sweet orange juice, and tart white wine. When the cooking liquid is reduced to a glaze to top the cooked artichoke wedges, the exotic nuances of the saffron shine through.

Tangy *pecorino romano* is a bright alternative to Parmesan when you want to keep a dish's flavor light. The crumbly yet creamy cheese is often paired with fresh mint, but using basil instead forms a pleasing contrast in the next recipe, a fast sauté of garden peas.

quick two-pea sauté with basil and pecorino

extra-virgin olive oil,
1 tablespoon

unsalted butter,
1 tablespoon

sugar snap peas,
½ pound, strings removed

english peas, 1 pound,
shelled

**sea salt and freshly
ground pepper**

lemon, 1

fresh basil, leaves from
4 sprigs, cut into thin
ribbons

pecorino romano cheese,
small chunk

MAKES 4 SERVINGS

In a large frying pan over medium heat, warm the oil and melt the butter. Add the snap peas and English peas. Pour in ¼ cup water and add a pinch of salt. Cover and cook for 2 minutes. Uncover and cook, stirring occasionally, until the water has evaporated, about 2 minutes longer. The peas should be tender-crisp and still bright green.

Finely grate 2 teaspoons zest from the lemon, then halve the lemon. Remove the pan from the heat and squeeze the juice from 1 lemon half over the peas (reserve the remaining half for another use). Add the lemon zest, basil, and a pinch each of salt and pepper to the pan. Grate some cheese over the top and stir well to mix.

Transfer the peas to a warmed serving dish and serve right away.

A speedy sauté brings out the natural sweetness of sugar snap peas and enhances their crunch. Fresh English peas, too, gain an intriguing sweetness from quick cooking. In this recipe, the vegetable cousins are tossed with anise-like fresh basil, tart lemon zest, and tangy pecorino cheese for a delicious, fast side dish.

summer

green beans with creamy tarragon dipping sauce

Whipping anise-scented tarragon and pleasantly tart crème fraîche until airy and light elevates this take on a crudité-and-dip platter. Cook the green beans until just tender, so their summer-fresh flavor is retained and they are firm enough to dip in the savory sauce.

Bring a saucepan of salted water to a boil. Fill a large bowl two-thirds full with ice water. Add the beans to the boiling water and cook until just tender, 4–5 minutes. Drain the beans and then immediately plunge them into the ice water. Let stand for a minute or two, then drain, pat dry, and arrange them on a serving platter.

In a bowl, combine the crème fraîche and heavy cream and whisk until the mixture is the texture of lightly whipped cream. Finely grate the lemon zest into the bowl, then halve the lemon and squeeze the juice from one half into the bowl (reserve the remaining half for another use). Add the tarragon to the crème fraîche mixture. Stir in the mustard and a pinch each of salt and pepper. Taste and adjust the seasonings.

Transfer the crème fraîche mixture to a small bowl and set on the platter with the beans for dipping. Serve right away.

green beans, 1 pound, stem ends trimmed

crème fraîche (page 142) or purchased, 1 cup

heavy cream, 2 tablespoons

lemon, 1

fresh tarragon, 1 teaspoon minced

dijon mustard, 1 teaspoon

sea salt and freshly ground pepper

MAKES 4 SERVINGS

grilled sweet corn with maple-cayenne butter

unsalted butter, ½ cup, at room temperature

pure maple syrup, grade b, 2 tablespoons

lemon, 1

cayenne pepper, pinch

sea salt and freshly ground black pepper

fresh sweet corn, 4 ears

canola oil

MAKES 4 SERVINGS

In a bowl, mix together the butter and maple syrup with a wooden spoon. Finely grate the zest from the lemon into the bowl. Halve the lemon and squeeze the juice from one half into the bowl (reserve the remaining half for another use). Mix well. Add the cayenne pepper and a pinch each of salt and black pepper and stir to blend. Taste and adjust the seasonings. Spoon the butter mixture onto a piece of plastic wrap and form it into a log about 1½ inches in diameter. Wrap the log tightly with the plastic wrap and refrigerate it until firm, about 1 hour.

Ten to twenty minutes before you plan to serve the corn, prepare a charcoal or gas grill for direct-heat grilling over high heat.

Shuck the corn, leaving a few leaves from the husks on, if desired, for a more rustic look. Rub each ear evenly with the oil and sprinkle lightly with salt, coating all sides. Grill the corn, turning occasionally, until browned in spots and tender, 12–14 minutes.

Transfer the corn ears to a warmed serving platter. Cut slices of butter from the log and place 1 slice on top of each ear, letting the butter melt and then spreading it over the corn, coating all sides. Serve right away. Pass the remaining maple-cayenne butter at the table.

Summer's fresh corn has a natural sweetness, which is nicely enhanced by the smoky flavors imparted by the grill. Grade B maple syrup boasts a complementary sugariness and a slight smokiness that serves as a counterpoint to the spicy cayenne in the rich butter topping.

Roasting heirloom tomatoes until their skins are charred concentrates their juices, drawing out their unique flavors. Toasted cubes of artisanal bread are perfect for soaking up the sweet-smoky tomato juices in a hearty salad.

bread salad with charred tomatoes, cucumber, and olives

country-style italian bread such as *pugliese*, ½ loaf (about 8 ounces)

ripe tomatoes, preferably in a mixture of colors, 4 large (about 2½ pounds total weight)

english cucumber, 1 small

red onion, ½, diced

kalamata olives, pitted and coarsely chopped, ¾ cup

extra-virgin olive oil, ⅓ cup

red wine vinegar, 2 tablespoons

sea salt and freshly ground pepper

fresh basil, ½ bunch

MAKES 4 SERVINGS

Preheat the oven to 375°F.

Cut the bread into ½-inch cubes and arrange them in a single layer on a baking sheet. Lightly toast in the oven until the cubes are just dry and very light brown, 8–10 minutes. Remove the cubes from the sheet and set aside.

Position an oven rack 6 inches below the heating element and preheat the broiler. Line a rimmed baking sheet with aluminum foil and place the tomatoes on the prepared sheet. Broil until the skins of the tomatoes begin to char and blacken, 2–3 minutes. Turn the tomatoes over and broil for 2–3 minutes longer, then remove from the oven and let cool.

When the tomatoes are cool enough to handle, remove and discard any loose skin, then coarsely chop and transfer the tomatoes to a large bowl (it's fine if a few charred bits of skin remain). Cut the cucumber in half lengthwise and scrape out the seeds. Cut the cucumber halves crosswise into slices about ½ inch thick and add them to the bowl with the tomatoes. Add the onion, olives, oil, vinegar, and a sprinkle each of salt and pepper to the the bowl and stir well to mix. Let stand at room temperature for up to 1 hour to blend the flavors.

Just before serving, add the toasted bread cubes to the vegetable mixture and toss gently. Pluck the leaves from the basil sprigs, tear them into small pieces, and add them to the bowl with the bread and tomatoes, tossing gently to mix. Taste and adjust the seasonings and serve right away.

Layering pungent, bitter, and salty ingredients is a great way to add dimension to vegetable dishes. Kalamata olives offer all three qualities, which makes them the perfect match for the smoky-sweet charred tomatoes, herbal-tinged cucumber, and crusty bread cubes in this creative summer salad.

spicy okra stew

This recipe uses seasonings popular in the eastern Mediterranean region, where aromatic coriander, musky cumin, and spicy cayenne are often used to flavor the cuisine. Parsley not only adds appealing, bright color, but lends the stew a fresh herbal taste that balances the earthy spices, crisp, hearty okra, and tart-sweet tomatoes.

Bring a small saucepan of water to a boil over high heat. Fill a large bowl two-thirds full with ice water. One at a time, lower the tomatoes into the boiling water and cook for 10 seconds. Immediately plunge each tomato into the ice water, let stand for a few seconds, and then drain the cooled tomatoes. Peel the skin from each tomato, then coarsely chop the flesh.

Remove the stems, and tails, if tough, from the okra and then cut the okra into slices about ¼ inch thick.

In a saucepan over medium heat, warm the oil. When the oil is hot, add the onion and a pinch of salt and sauté until the onion is just beginning to soften, 2–3 minutes. Add the okra and sauté until lightly browned, 7–10 minutes. Reduce the heat to medium-low and sauté until the okra is just tender, 4–5 minutes.

Add the garlic, cayenne, coriander, cumin, and a pinch each of salt and black pepper and cook for another minute to blend the flavors. Add the tomatoes and 1 cup water and simmer until the tomatoes have broken down and the mixture begins to thicken, 7–9 minutes. Taste and adjust the seasonings.

While the stew is cooking, pluck the leaves from the parsley sprigs and coarsely chop the leaves. Remove the stew from the heat and stir in the chopped parsley. Serve right away.

ripe tomatoes, 3 large

fresh okra, 1 pound

canola oil, 2 tablespoons

yellow onion, 1, diced

sea salt and freshly ground black pepper

garlic, 2 cloves, minced

cayenne pepper, ½ teaspoon

ground coriander, ½ teaspoon

ground cumin, ½ teaspoon

fresh flat-leaf parsley, ¼ bunch

MAKES 4 SERVINGS

A no-cook sauce made from ripe tomatoes, garlic, and fresh basil needs only a drizzle of high-quality olive oil for richness. You can use it over just about anything—grilled fish, cooked pasta, or paper-thin "noodles" of raw zucchini.

Keto

zucchini "pasta" with fresh tomato sauce

zucchini, 4 (about 2 pounds total weight)

sea salt and freshly ground pepper

ripe tomatoes, 4 large (about 2 pounds total weight), diced

garlic, 2 cloves, minced

fresh basil, leaves from ½ bunch, cut into thin ribbons

extra-virgin olive oil, 3 tablespoons

parmesan cheese, small chunk

MAKES 4 SERVINGS

Using a mandoline, sharp knife, or a very sharp vegetable peeler, cut each zucchini lengthwise into slices about ⅛ inch thick. Carefully place the slices in a large bowl, sprinkle with 1 tablespoon salt, and toss gently to coat. Line 1 or 2 baking sheets with paper towels. Transfer the salted zucchini slices to the prepared sheets, arranging them in a single layer, and let stand for 20 minutes. Turn the zucchini slices over and let stand for 10 minutes longer, then gently rinse under cold running water. Using a clean kitchen towel, pat the slices dry, then arrange them in a loose mound on a serving platter.

In a large bowl, combine the tomatoes with their juices, garlic, and basil and toss gently to mix. Stir 2 tablespoons of the oil and a generous pinch each of salt and pepper into the tomato mixture.

Drizzle the remaining 1 tablespoon oil over the zucchini and top with a few grinds of pepper. Spoon the tomato mixture evenly over the zucchini. Using a vegetable peeler, cut several shavings of Parmesan over the top of the dish. Serve right away.

Pasta-like ribbons of garden-fresh zucchini, a tangy raw tomato sauce, and thin shavings of parmesan give this familiar ingredient combination new life. Try to find Parmigiano-Reggiano straight from Italy, which will lend an especially nutty, almost caramel-like taste to this dish.

keto

sautéed yellow pear tomatoes with arugula pesto and feta

Buttery toasted walnuts and peppery arugula meld with the distinctive flavor of basil to create a bold version of pesto that coats a quick sauté of yellow pear tomatoes. Crumbled feta cheese lends its tangy richness to help bring all the tastes together.

Preheat the oven to 375°F.

Pour the walnuts onto a rimmed baking sheet. Toast the nuts in the oven until they turn a shade or two darker and are fragrant, 6–8 minutes. Pour the nuts onto a plate to cool.

Finely grate the zest from the lemon (reserve the fruit for another use). In the bowl of a food processor, combine the toasted walnuts, lemon zest, and garlic and pulse just to combine. Add the basil and arugula leaves and process until coarsely chopped. With the motor running, slowly pour in 4 tablespoons of the oil. Continue to process until the mixture is moist and well blended but still slightly chunky. Transfer the pesto to a small bowl and taste and adjust the seasonings with salt and pepper.

In a frying pan over medium-high heat, warm the remaining 1 tablespoon olive oil. When the oil is hot, add the tomatoes and a pinch of salt and sauté until the tomatoes are warmed through and their skins are just beginning to split, 3–4 minutes. Remove the pan from the heat and stir in the pesto.

Transfer the tomatoes to a serving dish and crumble the cheese over the top. Serve hot or at room temperature.

walnuts, 3 tablespoons

lemon, 1

garlic, 1 clove, roughly chopped

fresh basil leaves, from ¼ bunch

baby arugula leaves, 1 cup packed

extra-virgin olive oil, 5 tablespoons

sea salt and freshly ground pepper

yellow pear tomatoes, 1½ pounds

feta cheese, 2 ounces

MAKES 4 SERVINGS

Keto

spicy cucumber salad with roasted peanuts

rice vinegar, ⅓ cup

sugar, 1½ tablespoons

sea salt and freshly ground pepper

english cucumber, 1

red onion, ¼, thinly sliced

jalapeño chile, 1, thinly sliced

fresh cilantro, leaves from ¼ bunch

roasted peanuts, 2 tablespoons

MAKES 4 SERVINGS

In a small nonreactive saucepan, combine the vinegar, sugar, and a pinch each of salt and pepper. Bring to a boil over medium-high heat, then reduce the heat to low. Cook, stirring occasionally, until the sugar dissolves, 2–3 minutes. Remove from the heat and let cool completely.

While the vinegar mixture is cooling, cut the cucumber into slices about ¼ inch thick and place them in a large bowl with the onion and chile. Pour the vinegar mixture over the vegetables and stir well to coat. Let the vegetables stand at room temperature for at least 30 minutes, stirring it occasionally, to blend the flavors.

Just before serving, coarsely chop the cilantro and the peanuts. Stir the cilantro into the salad. Transfer the salad to a serving dish and top with the peanuts. Serve at room temperature.

A sprinkle of toasted peanuts and bright cilantro contributes an intriguing dimension to this Thai-style salad, which is refreshing, pungent, and spicy at the same time. Marinating the cucumber, onion, and chile in the sweetened vinegar mixture mellows their distinctive flavors and softens their textures.

Roasting poblano chiles brings out a natural sweetness and contributes a subtle smokiness. Adding chopped chile to the vegetable mixture that fills whole chiles reinforces the flavor. Poblanos vary in their heat, so every bite holds a surprise.

poblano chiles stuffed with black beans and summer squash

poblano chiles, 8

extra-virgin olive oil,
2 tablespoons

white onion, ½, finely
diced

**sea salt and freshly ground
black pepper**

zucchini, 1, diced

yellow summer squash,
2, diced

ripe tomato, 1, diced

cayenne pepper,
¼ teaspoon

black beans, 1 can
(15 ounces), drained
and rinsed

fresh cilantro, leaves from
¼ bunch, coarsely chopped

**cooked white rice
(page 142),** 1 cup

**crème fraîche (page 142 or
purchased),** ½ cup

parmesan cheese,
small chunk

MAKES 4–6 SERVINGS

Position an oven rack 6 inches below the heating element and preheat the broiler. Line a rimmed baking sheet with aluminum foil and place 2 of the chiles on the prepared sheet. Broil the chiles, turning occasionally, until charred on all sides, about 15 minutes. Set the oven temperature to 400°F. Transfer the chiles to a bowl, cover tightly with plastic wrap, and let steam for 5 minutes. With wet fingers, pull off the skin from the chiles. Remove the seeds and stems from the chiles, dice the flesh, and set aside.

Cut a 2-inch-long slit in each of the remaining 6 chiles. With a paring knife, carefully scrape out the seeds from the insides of the chiles.

In a sauté pan over medium heat, warm the oil. When the oil is hot, add the onion and a pinch of salt and sauté until the onion is soft and translucent, 5–6 minutes. Add the zucchini and summer squash, cover the pan, and sauté until just tender, 5–6 minutes. Uncover, add the tomato, cayenne, and a pinch each of salt and pepper and sauté for 2 minutes. Remove the pan from the heat and let the vegetables cool slightly.

Add the beans, cilantro, rice, and crème fraîche to the pan and mix well. Spoon the bean mixture into the chiles, dividing it evenly. Place the stuffed chiles, cut side up, in a baking dish, and add enough water to come ½ inch up the sides of the dish. Cover tightly with aluminum foil and bake until the stuffing is heated through and the water has evaporated, about 20 minutes. Remove the foil, grate some cheese over the tops of the chiles, and bake, uncovered, until the cheese melts, about 5 minutes.

Serve right away directly from the baking dish.

Broiling chiles until their skins blacken imparts an alluring smokiness. Here, zucchini, summer squash, and roasted chiles are added to the hearty black-bean-and-rice filling, which is stuffed into whole chiles for a light, summery dish. Tangy crème fraîche and salty Parmesan add refreshing accents.

marinated summer vegetables grilled on rosemary skewers

Garden-fresh summer vegetables need little to adorn them. Here, they're marinated in a simple vinaigrette, then threaded onto sturdy rosemary stems and grilled over a hot fire. This unique cooking process infuses smoky-woodsy nuances into the vegetables as the herb stems smolder over the high heat of the grill.

Cut the eggplant lengthwise into quarters, then cut each quarter into slices about ½ inch thick. Cut the zucchini into rounds about ½ inch thick.

Add the garlic to a large bowl. Pluck the leaves from 1 rosemary sprig and add them to the bowl. Add the mustard, oil, vinegar, and a pinch each of salt and pepper and stir well. Add the eggplant and zucchini slices, and the tomatoes, and toss well to coat. Cover the bowl with plastic wrap and let the vegetables marinate at room temperature for 1 hour.

Meanwhile, strip the leaves from the bottom two-thirds of the remaining 8 rosemary sprigs (reserve the leaves for another use). Place the sprigs in a shallow dish, add water to cover, and soak for 1 hour to prevent them from burning on the grill.

Drain the rosemary sprigs. Thread the vegetables onto the sprigs, alternating the eggplant slices, zucchini slices, and tomatoes, and shaking off any excess marinade as you remove the vegetables from the bowl. Reserve the marinade.

Ten to twenty minutes before you plan to serve the vegetable skewers, prepare a charcoal or gas grill for direct-heat grilling over high heat. Grill the vegetables, turning once or twice, until the vegetables are tender but not falling apart, 8–10 minutes. Transfer to a serving platter and drizzle with the remaining marinade. Serve hot or at room temperature.

globe eggplant, 1 small (about 1 pound)

zucchini, 1

garlic, 1 clove, minced

fresh rosemary sprigs, 9 large, with strong, woody stems

dijon mustard, 1 teaspoon

extra-virgin olive oil, ⅓ cup

sherry vinegar, 1 tablespoon

sea salt and freshly ground pepper

cherry tomatoes, 1 pint

MAKES 4 SERVINGS

creamed corn with chipotle chiles

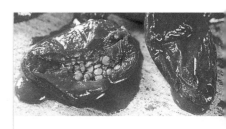

fresh sweet corn, 6 ears

unsalted butter,
2 tablespoons

white onion, ½, finely
diced

**chipotle chiles in adobo
sauce,** 2, seeded and
minced, plus 1 teaspoon
adobo sauce

dried mexican oregano,
1 teaspoon

sugar, ½ teaspoon

**sea salt and freshly
ground pepper**

heavy cream, ¾ cup

MAKES 4 SERVINGS

Remove the husks and silk from the corn. Using a large, sharp knife, carefully cut the ear in half crosswise. One at a time, stand the halves, flat end down, on a cutting board and cut the kernels from the cob. Transfer the kernels to a bowl. Using the dull edge of a knife, carefully scrape the wet pulp from the corn cobs into the bowl.

In a large sauté pan over medium heat, melt the butter. Add the onion and sauté until soft and translucent, 5–6 minutes. Add the chipotle chiles, adobo sauce, corn kernels with pulp, oregano, and sugar. Pour in ½ cup water and add a generous pinch each of salt and pepper. Bring the mixture to a boil, reduce the heat to low, cover, and cook, stirring occasionally, until the corn is tender but still has a bit of crunch, 10 minutes. Uncover and cook until the water evaporates, 2–3 minutes.

Add the cream to the pan, raise the heat to medium-low, and cook until the liquid is thick enough to coat the back of a spoon, 2–3 minutes. Taste and adjust the seasonings.

Transfer the corn to a warmed serving bowl and serve right away.

Naturally sweet summer corn contrasts beautifully with spicy and smoky ingredients, such as the chipotle chiles used here. Rich, silky heavy cream lends a complementary sweetness and pleasing richness to the dish and prevents the spice of the chiles from overwhelming the other ingredients.

Miso is to Japanese cooking what mustard is to French cuisine—a versatile flavoring for sauces, marinades, and glazes. In the following recipe, miso enlivens a sweet basting glaze that boosts the delicate taste of Asian eggplant.

miso-glazed grilled asian eggplant

Ginger, garlic, and green onions are fundamental ingredients in Asian cooking. Together they provide a flavor base onto which other ingredients, here, savory miso, spicy pepper sauce, and tart rice vinegar, can be layered. Slender Asian eggplant, cut lengthwise, offers an exposed surface into which the miso basting sauce can absorb and the smoke from the grill can penetrate.

In a blender, combine the ginger, garlic, miso, pepper sauce, vinegar, sugar, mirin, and 1 tablespoon water. Blend to form a smooth purée.

Cut each eggplant in half lengthwise and sprinkle lightly with salt and pepper. Lightly brush the eggplant halves all over with the oil.

Ten to twenty minutes before you plan to serve the eggplant, prepare a charcoal or gas grill for direct-heat grilling over medium-high heat. Place the eggplant halves, cut side down, on the grill, cover the grill, and cook until the flesh just starts to char and soften, 6–8 minutes. Turn the eggplant over and cook, covered, until just tender, 3–4 minutes longer. Brush the cut sides of the eggplant with the miso mixture and cook, covered, until the eggplant is tender and the glaze has browned in spots, 3–4 minutes.

Cut the green onions on the diagonal into ¼-inch slices. Transfer the eggplant to a warmed serving platter, sprinkle with the sliced green onions, and serve right away.

fresh ginger, ¼-inch piece, peeled and coarsely chopped

garlic, 1 clove, coarsely chopped

white miso, ¼ cup

hot red-pepper sauce such as sriracha, ½ teaspoon

rice vinegar, 2 tablespoons

sugar, 2 teaspoons

mirin, 1 tablespoon

asian eggplants, 4

sea salt and freshly ground pepper

canola oil

green onions, 3

MAKES 4 SERVINGS

fall

potato–celery root pancakes

russet potatoes, 2 small
(about 1 pound)

celery root, 1 (about
½ pound)

shallot, 1, minced

large eggs, 2

all-purpose flour,
2 tablespoons

sea salt and freshly
ground pepper

canola oil

coarse sea salt

MAKES 4–6 SERVINGS

Peel the potatoes and celery root. Using a food processor fitted with the shredding blade, shred the potatoes and celery root. (Alternatively, shred the vegetables using the large holes of a box grater-shredder.) Line a colander with cheesecloth or a thin kitchen towel. Transfer the potatoes and celery root to the colander, set over a bowl, and twist the cheesecloth tightly into a pouch, squeezing out the moisture. Let the vegetables drain for 15 minutes. Squeeze the cheesecloth again. Carefully pour out the clear liquid from the bowl, leaving behind the white starchy substance that settles in the bottom of the bowl.

Add the shallot, eggs, flour, 1½ teaspoons salt, and 1½ teaspoons pepper to the bowl and beat with a fork until well blended. Add the shredded potatoes and celery root and toss to combine.

Preheat the oven to 200°F. Line a baking sheet with paper towels.

Heat a large nonstick frying pan with high sides over medium-high heat. Pour in enough oil to reach ¼ inch up the sides of the pan. When the oil begins to shimmer, carefully drop heaping tablespoonfuls of the potato mixture into the pan, spacing each portion 1 inch apart. Using a spatula, gently press on the pancakes to flatten them and cook, turning once, until they are golden and crisp, 3–4 minutes per side. Transfer the pancakes to the towel-lined baking sheet and keep warm in the oven. Repeat to cook the remaining potato mixture.

Sprinkle the pancakes with coarse sea salt and serve right away.

Crisp, salty potato patties are updated with tangy celery root for a unique take on a classic dish. Choose a high-quality sea salt for sprinkling, which will contribute an appealing briny taste and additional crunch to the pancakes.

Keto

stir-fried broccoli with cashews and dark soy sauce

Dark soy sauce has a molasses-like consistency and adds both sweetness and heartiness to this dish. Mirin lends a measure of brightness, oyster sauce an intriguing savory flavor, and cashews a delightful nuttiness. Together, they're a tasty way to perk up pleasantly bitter broccoli florets in a quick stir-fry.

Preheat the oven to 375°F.

Pour the cashews onto a rimmed baking sheet. Toast the cashews in the oven until they turn a shade or two darker and are fragrant, 6–8 minutes. Pour onto a plate to cool.

In a small bowl, combine the broth, oyster sauce, dark soy sauce, and mirin. Stir well, then add the cornstarch and stir to dissolve.

In a wok or a large frying pan over medium-high heat, warm the oil. When the oil is hot and shimmering in the pan, add the broccoli. Cook, tossing and stirring constantly, until the broccoli is well coated with oil and is vibrant green, about 3 minutes. Add the garlic and cook, stirring, for 1 minute. Add the soy sauce mixture, bring to a boil, and cook, tossing, until the sauce thickens and the broccoli is tender-crisp, about 4 minutes.

Add the cashews and stir well. Transfer the broccoli mixture to a warmed serving dish and serve right away.

cashews, 1/3 cup

low-sodium chicken broth, 1/2 cup

oyster sauce, 2 tablespoons

dark soy sauce, 2 tablespoons

mirin, 2 tablespoons

cornstarch, 1 teaspoon

olive ~~**canola**~~ **oil,** 2 tablespoons

broccoli, 1 head (about 1 pound), cut into 1-inch florets

garlic, 1 clove, minced

MAKES 4 SERVINGS

Beets have a distinctive flavor that evokes the freshly turned soil from which they are dug. They really shine in preparations that utilize contrasting, brightly flavored ingredients, such as the herb-flecked goat cheese that adorns them here.

roasted beets with orange and herbed goat cheese

A trio of fresh herbs accents the tangy flavor of soft goat cheese. Dollops of the mixture nicely offset a salad of just-harvested beets, whose earthiness becomes even more intense when roasted in a hot oven. The beet juices are blended with tart fresh orange juice to form a colorful dressing to bring all the tastes together.

Preheat the oven to 400°F.

Finely grate the zest from the orange and set aside. Halve the orange and place one half in a baking dish just large enough to hold it and the beets in a single layer. Add the beets and drizzle with 2 tablespoons of the oil. Add the garlic cloves, sprinkle lightly with salt and pepper, and toss well. Cover the dish with aluminum foil and roast until the beets are tender when pierced with a sharp knife, about 45 minutes.

In a small bowl, stir together the goat cheese, chives, parsley, tarragon, and a pinch each of salt and pepper. Refrigerate until serving.

Remove the beets from the oven and let cool. Using the dull side of a paring knife, gently scrape off the beet skins, then cut the beets into slices about ¼ inch thick. Arrange the slices on a platter. Reserve the cooking liquid.

Line a strainer with a damp paper towel and place over a bowl. Pour the cooking liquid through the strainer, squeezing the orange half to release any juice. Whisk in the remaining 1 tablespoon oil and the juice from the remaining orange half to make a dressing. Taste and adjust the seasonings. Let the dressing cool to room temperature.

Drizzle the beets lightly with the dressing, then sprinkle lightly with salt and pepper. Top the beets with small spoonfuls of the herbed goat cheese, garnish with the orange zest, and serve right away.

orange, 1

beets, 6 (about 1½ pounds total weight), in assorted colors, greens removed

extra-virgin olive oil, 3 tablespoons

garlic, 2 cloves

sea salt and freshly ground pepper

fresh goat cheese, 2 ounces

fresh chives, 1½ teaspoons minced

fresh flat-leaf parsley, 1½ teaspoons minced

fresh tarragon, ½ teaspoon minced

MAKES 4 SERVINGS

wasabi-chive mashed potatoes

russet potatoes, 4 large (about 3½ pounds total weight)

sea salt and freshly ground pepper

unsalted butter, 4 tablespoons

heavy cream, ½ cup

milk, ½ cup

wasabi paste or powder, 2–3 teaspoons

fresh chives, ¼ cup minced

MAKES 4 SERVINGS

Peel the potatoes, cut them into quarters, and place them in a saucepan. Add a generous pinch of salt and enough cold water to cover the potatoes. Bring the water to a boil over high heat, reduce the heat to low, and cook until the potatoes are tender when pierced with a sharp knife but not falling apart, 20–30 minutes.

Meanwhile, in a small saucepan over medium-low heat, warm the butter, cream, and milk, stirring to melt the butter. Add 2 teaspoons of the wasabi paste and a pinch each of salt and pepper and stir well. Taste and adjust the seasonings, adding the additional 1 teaspoon wasabi paste if you prefer a bolder, spicier flavor.

Drain the potatoes and return them to the hot pan. Place the pan over medium heat and cook for 1–2 minutes to eliminate any remaining moisture. Transfer the potatoes to the bowl of a stand mixer fitted with the paddle attachment, and mix on low speed just to break them up. Gradually increase the speed to medium and continue to mix. When the potatoes are almost smooth, turn off the mixer and add half of the warm milk mixture. Mix on medium speed to blend, adding more of the milk mixture as needed to achieve a creamy consistency.

Stir the chives into the potatoes, then taste and adjust the seasonings with salt and pepper. Serve right away.

Potent wasabi paste elevates plain mashed potatoes to something really special——just a couple of teaspoons adds a lot of fire. Oniony fresh chives lend another boost of flavor as well as vibrant green color. Rich cream and silky butter help all the ingredients shine.

Popular in the cooking of Southern Italy, broccoli rabe, or *rapini,* has a pleasantly bitter taste. Oil-packed anchovies, another regional ingredient, help balance the pungency of the vegetable with their unique salty-meaty-nutty flavor.

sautéed broccoli rabe with garlic, anchovies, and red pepper flakes

broccoli rabe, 1 bunch
(about 1½ pounds)

extra-virgin olive oil,
¼ cup, plus oil for drizzling

garlic, 2 cloves, thinly sliced

**oil-packed anchovy
fillets,** 2, minced

red pepper flakes,
½ teaspoon

**sea salt and freshly
ground pepper**

lemon, 1

MAKES 4 SERVINGS

Bring a large pot of salted water to a boil over high heat. Fill a large bowl two-thirds full with ice water.

Trim off any tough stems and wilted leaves from the broccoli rabe and discard. Cut the leaves and stems into 1- to 2-inch pieces. Add the broccoli rabe to the boiling water and cook for 2 minutes. Drain the broccoli rabe and immediately plunge it into the ice water. Let stand for a minute or two, then drain the cooled broccoli rabe and set aside.

In a large frying pan over medium heat, warm the ¼ cup oil. When the oil is hot, add the garlic, anchovies, and red pepper flakes and sauté just until the garlic is fragrant, about 1 minute. Do not let the garlic brown.

Add the broccoli rabe, with the water still clinging to the leaves, to the pan and cook, tossing constantly with tongs, until it begins to wilt, about 2 minutes. Add a generous pinch each of salt and pepper, toss, and reduce the heat to medium-low. Simmer until the broccoli rabe is tender-crisp, about 3 minutes longer.

Transfer the broccoli rabe mixture to a warmed serving dish. Halve the lemon and squeeze the juice from one half over the broccoli rabe, then drizzle with oil. Cut the remaining lemon half into wedges. Serve the broccoli rabe right away with the lemon wedges on the side for squeezing.

Toasting garlic in olive oil softens its pungency and draws out a natural nuttiness. Here, it is combined with salty anchovies and spicy red pepper flakes to help temper the slightly bitter taste of broccoli rabe. Italian white anchovies, or alici, *have a pleasing, mild, salty flavor, so use them in this dish if you can find them.*

roasted acorn squash with chipotle and cilantro

Herbal cilantro and tart lime juice help cut through the creaminess of the squash. Spicy and smoky chipotle chiles, too, are a delightful contrast to the sweet autumn vegetable. The result is a balanced dish that's not too spicy, with many layers of intriguing flavor.

Preheat the oven to 425°F.

Cut each squash in half, then scoop out and discard the seeds. Cut each half into crescent-shaped wedges about ¾ inch thick.

Halve one of the limes and squeeze the juice into a large bowl. Add the oil, adobo sauce, sugar, and a pinch each of salt and pepper and stir well. Add the squash wedges to the bowl and toss well to coat. Pour the wedges and their juices onto 1 or 2 baking sheets and arrange them in a single layer. Roast, turning once, until the squash is golden brown and tender when pierced with a sharp knife, about 25 minutes.

While the squash is roasting, remove the seeds from the chile, then mince. Cut the remaining lime into wedges.

Transfer the squash wedges to a large bowl. Add the minced chile and the cilantro and toss well to coat. Arrange the squash on a warmed platter, garnish with the lime wedges, and serve right away.

acorn squash, 2

limes, 2

extra-virgin olive oil, 3 tablespoons

chipotle chile in adobo sauce, 1, plus 1 teaspoon adobo sauce

sugar, ½ teaspoon

sea salt and freshly ground pepper

fresh cilantro, 2 tablespoons coarsely chopped

MAKES 4 SERVINGS

keto

caramelized cauliflower with honey and smoked paprika

extra-virgin olive oil,
3 tablespoons

unsalted butter,
2 tablespoons

cauliflower, 1 large head,
(about 3 pounds) cut into
1-inch florets

**sea salt and freshly
ground pepper**

shallot, 1, minced

red pepper flakes,
¼ teaspoon

smoked sweet paprika,
½ teaspoon

honey, 2 tablespoons

lemon, ½

MAKES 4 SERVINGS

In a large frying pan over medium heat, warm 2 tablespoons of the oil and melt the butter. Add the cauliflower florets, sprinkle with a generous pinch of salt, and toss gently to coat the florets. Spread the florets into 1 layer and cook, without stirring, until the undersides are lightly browned, 3–4 minutes. Flip each piece over and continue cooking, undisturbed, until evenly browned, 3–4 minutes. Repeat until all sides are evenly browned, 3–5 minutes longer.

Add the remaining 1 tablespoon oil, the shallot, red pepper flakes, and paprika to the pan. Cook, stirring occasionally, until the shallot is softened, 2–3 minutes. Add the honey and 2 tablespoons water and sauté until the liquid reduces to a glaze, 2–3 minutes. Squeeze the juice from the lemon half over the cauliflower, stir to combine, and cook for 30 seconds. Remove from the heat. Taste and adjust the seasonings with salt and pepper.

Transfer the cauliflower to a warmed bowl and serve right away.

Cooking the cauliflower in a smoking-hot pan until well browned elicits a natural sweetness normally not found in cauliflower dishes. This dark, caramel-like flavor is enhanced by the honey-based glaze and punched up with smoky paprika, spicy chile flakes, and tart fresh lemon juice.

glazed carrots with coriander

Lightly toasted coriander seeds bring hints of lemon, sage, and caraway to this dish. Cilantro, the fresh herb born of the coriander seed, adds a complementary freshness and sets off the honey-lemon glaze that coats the naturally sweet carrots.

Peel the carrots, then cut them on the diagonal into slices ¼ inch thick.

In a small frying pan over medium heat, toast the coriander seeds, shaking the pan occasionally, until the seeds are a shade or two darker and fragrant, about 1 minute. Remove the pan from the heat and transfer the seeds to a spice grinder or mortar and pestle and grind to a fine powder.

In a frying pan over medium heat, melt the butter. Add the ground coriander and cook, stirring occasionally, until fragrant, about 1 minute. Squeeze the juice from the lemon half into the pan, add the honey and ⅔ cup water and sauté for 1 minute. Add the carrots, a pinch each of salt and pepper, and stir well. Raise the heat to medium-high and cook, stirring occasionally, until the carrots are just tender and the liquid is reduced to a glaze, 12–15 minutes. If the carrots are still not tender after the liquid has reduced, add a bit more water to the pan and continue to cook.

Stir the cilantro into the carrots, then taste and adjust the seasonings. Transfer to a warmed serving dish and serve right away.

carrots, preferably a mixture of colors, 2 pounds

whole coriander seeds, 1 teaspoon

unsalted butter, 4 tablespoons

lemon, ½

honey, 3 tablespoons

sea salt and freshly ground pepper

fresh cilantro, 2 tablespoons coarsely chopped

MAKES 4 SERVINGS

Cranberry beans, with their bright pink-and-white speckles, are a feast for the eyes as well as the palate. Their mild flavor, like many shelling beans, is nicely complemented by smoked bacon. Thick-cut varieties provide the most impact.

shell beans with butternut squash, bacon, and sage

Woodsy fresh sage pairs nicely with a variety of autumnal ingredients, like creamy-textured cubes of sweet butternut squash and earthy-tasting shelling beans. Toasted nuts and salty bacon lend welcome contrasting flavors and textures to round out the dish.

Preheat the oven to 375°F.

Pour the pecans onto a rimmed baking sheet. Toast in the oven until they turn a shade or two darker and are fragrant, 6–8 minutes. Pour the nuts onto a plate to cool.

Bring a large saucepan of water to a boil over high heat. Add the beans to the boiling water, reduce the heat to medium, and simmer until the beans are tender but not falling apart, 25–30 minutes. Make sure that the water is always about an inch above the beans. Drain the beans and set aside.

Peel the squash, then cut it in half lengthwise and scoop out and discard the seeds. Cut the flesh into ½-inch dice.

Heat a nonstick frying pan over medium heat. Add the bacon slices and cook, turning once, until browned and crisp, 7–9 minutes. Transfer the bacon to paper towels to drain. Pour off all but 1 tablespoon of the bacon fat from the pan. When the bacon has cooled, cut it crosswise into ¼-inch pieces.

Return the frying pan to the stove top over medium-high heat. Add the squash and cook, stirring frequently, until lightly browned and just tender when pierced with a sharp knife, 5–7 minutes. Add the sage and beans, drizzle with oil, and sprinkle lightly with salt and pepper. Cook, stirring frequently, until the beans are heated through and the flavors are blended, about 1 minute. Stir in the bacon and pecans.

Transfer the mixture to a warmed platter and serve right away.

pecan halves, ¼ cup

fresh shell beans such as cranberry beans, 1 pound, shelled

butternut squash, 1 small (about 1½ pounds)

high-quality, thick-sliced bacon, 2 slices

fresh sage, 1½ tablespoons minced

extra-virgin olive oil for drizzling

sea salt and freshly ground pepper

MAKES 4 SERVINGS

mushroom and potato gratin with thyme and parmesan

unsalted butter,
1 tablespoon, plus more
for greasing

heavy cream, 1½ cups

garlic, 1 clove, thinly sliced

fresh thyme, 3 sprigs, plus
1½ teaspoons minced

**sea salt and freshly
ground pepper**

yukon gold potatoes,
2 pounds

extra-virgin olive oil,
1 tablespoon

**mixed wild and cultivated
mushrooms,** 1 pound,
woody stems removed,
thinly sliced

parmesan cheese,
4 tablespoons grated

MAKES 4–6 SERVINGS

Preheat the oven to 375°F. Butter an 8-inch square baking dish.

In a saucepan, combine the cream, garlic, thyme sprigs, and a pinch each of salt and pepper. Bring to a low boil over medium heat, then remove from the heat and set aside.

Peel the potatoes, and, using a mandoline or a very sharp knife, cut them into slices about ⅛ inch thick. Gently stir the potato slices into the cream mixture, cover, and let stand while you cook the mushrooms.

In a frying pan over medium heat, warm the olive oil and melt the 1 tablespoon butter. Add the mushrooms and a pinch of salt and sauté until all of the liquid released by the mushrooms has evaporated, 7–9 minutes. Add the minced thyme with a pinch of pepper and cook for 1 minute.

Arrange one-third of the potato slices, slightly overlapping, on the bottom of the prepared dish. Sprinkle lightly with salt and pepper and 1 tablespoon of the Parmesan. Spread half of the mushrooms over the potatoes and sprinkle with another 1 tablespoon Parmesan. Repeat these layers, using half of the remaining potatoes and all of the remaining mushrooms, and sprinkling with salt, pepper, and 1 tablespoon Parmesan between the layers of vegetables. Top with the remaining potatoes and sprinkle with salt and pepper. Using a large, flat spatula, gently press on the vegetables to compact them. Pour the cream mixture through a strainer into the dish and sprinkle with the remaining 1 tablespoon Parmesan.

Cover the dish with aluminum foil and bake until the potatoes are tender when pierced with a sharp knife, about 45 minutes. Remove the foil and bake until the mixture is golden brown and bubbly, about 20 minutes longer. Let the gratin rest for about 10 minutes, then use a sharp-bladed spatula to cut it into squares and serve right away.

Using a combination of wild and cultivated mushrooms, such as chanterelle, cremini, and white button, gives this gratin a deep earthiness that enhances the buttery Yukon gold potatoes. Savory garlic, luxurious cream, fragrant thyme, and salty Parmesan bring increased dimension to the dish.

At farmers' markets in the fall, you can find carrots in a rainbow of colors and a variety of shapes. Mixed with other root vegetables and roasted with robust curry powder, they become an exotic take on herb-roasted potatoes.

roasted root vegetables with indian curry and cilantro

carrots, 5 (about 1 pound total weight)

parsnips, 2 or 3 (about 1 pound total weight)

turnip, 1 or 2 (about 1 pound total weight)

red onion, 1 large

madras curry powder, 1½ teaspoons

extra-virgin olive oil, ¼ cup

sea salt and freshly ground pepper

garlic, 8 large cloves

fresh cilantro, 3 tablespoons coarsely chopped

MAKES 4 SERVINGS

Preheat the oven to 500°F.

Peel the carrots, parsnips, and turnip and cut them into 1-inch pieces. Cut the onion into 2-inch chunks.

In a frying pan over medium heat, toast the curry powder, shaking the pan occasionally, until fragrant, about 1 minute. Remove the pan from the heat and immediately transfer the curry powder to a large bowl. Stir the oil and a generous pinch each of salt and pepper into the curry powder. Add the carrots, parsnips, turnip, onion, and garlic, and toss well to coat.

Arrange the vegetables in a single layer on 1 or 2 rimmed baking sheets. Roast the vegetables , turning them once after 15 minutes, until they are just tender when pierced with a sharp knife, about 30 minutes.

Transfer the roasted vegetables to a warmed serving dish, sprinkle with the cilantro, and stir gently to combine. Serve right away.

Toasting curry powder and then mixing it with oil intensifies its multilayered taste. It nicely contrasts with earthy root vegetables, which are roasted in a hot oven to coax out their natural sweetness. A sprinkle of bright-tasting cilantro lends a refreshing component to the dish.

winter

spicy roasted potatoes with cool yogurt dipping sauce

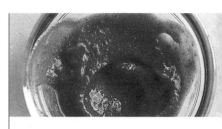

canola oil, ¼ cup

russet potatoes, 3 pounds

prepared harissa,
2 tablespoons

cayenne pepper,
¼ teaspoon

sesame seeds,
1 tablespoon

**sea salt and freshly ground
black pepper**

greek-style plain yogurt,
1 cup

fresh mint, leaves from
½ bunch

lemon, ½

MAKES 4 SERVINGS

Preheat the oven to 425°F. Drizzle the oil into the bottom of a roasting pan and place the pan in the oven as it preheats.

Peel the potatoes, then cut them into 2-inch chunks. In a large bowl, combine the harissa, cayenne, sesame seeds, and 1 teaspoon salt. Add the potatoes and toss to coat the potatoes well.

When the roasting pan is hot, remove it from the oven and carefully add the potatoes, tossing gently to coat the potatoes in the oil. Arrange the potatoes in a single layer in the pan. Roast until the undersides of the potato chunks are nicely browned, 25–30 minutes. Using a metal spatula, flip the potatoes and roast until tender inside and browned and crisp outside, about 15 minutes longer.

While the potatoes are roasting, add the yogurt to a small bowl. Cut the mint into thin ribbons and fold it into the yogurt. Squeeze the juice from the lemon half into the yogurt and mix well. Taste and adjust the seasonings with salt and black pepper.

Transfer the roasted potatoes to a warmed platter and serve right away with the yogurt sauce on the side for dipping.

North African harissa perks up plain russet potato chunks with its spicy, exotic taste. Cayenne pepper adds another layer of heat and sesame seeds gild the vegetables with their toasty, nutty flavor. To counter the boldness of the potatoes, they are dipped into a cooling sauce of creamy, tangy, Greek-style yogurt enhanced with lemon juice and fresh mint.

braised black kale with white beans and smoked ham

High-quality ham contributes a smoky, meaty flavor that mimics long cooking in this quick braise of peppery black kale, or cavalo nero. Creamy, earthy beans, and woodsy fresh rosemary combine to create a satisfying dish that can even be served as a main course.

Strip the stalks and ribs from the kale leaves and discard, then tear the leaves into 2-inch pieces. Drain the beans, rinse them, and drain again.

In a frying pan over medium-low heat, warm the oil. When the oil is hot, add the garlic and sauté until lightly browned, about 1 minute. Add the ham and sauté for 1 minute longer. Add the kale, cover the pan, and cook, turning occasionally, until the kale leaves just begin to wilt, 2–3 minutes. Add the broth and a pinch each of salt and pepper and cook until the leaves are just tender and the liquid has almost evaporated, 4–5 minutes.

Add the beans and rosemary to the pan and raise the heat to medium-high. Cook, tossing gently, until the beans are heated through, 2–3 minutes. Taste and adjust the seasonings and serve right away.

black kale, 2 bunches (about 1 pound total weight)

cannellini beans, 1 can (15 ounces)

extra-virgin olive oil, 2 teaspoons

garlic, 2 cloves, thinly sliced

smoked ham such as black forest, 4 ounces, diced

low-sodium chicken broth, ½ cup

sea salt and freshly ground pepper

fresh rosemary, ½ teaspoon minced

MAKES 4 SERVINGS

The freshest Brussels sprouts, found in markets in the fall and winter, are those still clinging to their thick stalks. Nuts are the vegetable's classic partner, and chestnuts, with their sweet flavor and chewy texture, are a luxurious choice.

vinegar-glazed brussels sprouts with chestnuts and walnut oil

brussels sprouts, 1 pound

extra-virgin olive oil, 1 tablespoon

sea salt and freshly ground pepper

unsalted butter, 1 tablespoon

low-sodium chicken broth, 1 cup

purchased, steamed chestnuts, ½ cup (about 3 ounces), coarsely chopped

light brown sugar, 1 tablespoon

red wine vinegar, 2 tablespoons

roasted walnut oil, 2 teaspoons

MAKES 4 SERVINGS

Trim the bases of the Brussels sprouts and remove and discard any blemished or discolored leaves.

In a large frying pan over medium heat, warm the olive oil. When the olive oil is hot, add the Brussels sprouts in a single layer and sprinkle lightly with salt. Cook, stirring once or twice, until the Brussels sprouts are golden brown and caramelized on all sides, about 4 minutes.

Raise the heat to medium-high and add the butter, broth, and chestnuts to the pan. Bring the broth to a boil and, using a wooden spoon, scrape up any browned bits from the bottom of the pan. Reduce the heat to medium-low and simmer, partially covered, until the sprouts are just tender when pierced with a sharp knife and most of the liquid has evaporated, 20–22 minutes.

Add ¼ cup of water to the pan, stir in the sugar and vinegar, and raise the heat to medium-high. Cook, stirring occasionally, until the liquid reduces to a glaze, 2–3 minutes. Remove the pan from the heat and stir in the walnut oil. Taste and adjust the seasonings with salt and pepper.

Transfer to a warmed serving bowl and serve right away.

In this dish, the potent nuttiness of walnut oil as well as sweet brown sugar and tart wine vinegar work together to counter the bitterness of cabbage-like Brussels sprouts. Chestnuts contribute another layer of nuttiness and a pleasing meaty texture.

gingered winter squash and pear purée

Preheat the oven to 400°F. Lightly grease 2 rimmed baking sheets.

Cut the squash in half lengthwise, then scoop out the seeds and discard. Peel the pears, halve them, then remove the cores with a paring knife or melon baller. Brush the cut sides of the squash and pears with the 2 tablespoons oil and sprinkle lightly with salt and pepper. Place the squash, cut sides down, on one of the prepared sheets. Place the pears, cut sides down, on the other sheet. Cover the baking sheets with aluminum foil and roast until the squash and pears are very tender when pierced with a sharp knife, 30–35 minutes for the pears and 1 hour for the squash.

Place the cooked pears in the bowl of a stand mixer fitted with the paddle attachment. When the squash is cool enough to handle, scoop out the flesh and add it to the bowl with the pears. Discard the squash skins. Mix on medium speed until smooth. It is okay if a few coarse pieces of pear remain, but the squash should be completely smooth.

In a saucepan over medium heat, melt the butter, stirring occasionally, until it just begins to brown and smell nutty, 4–5 minutes. Stir in the ginger and sage and cook, stirring, for 1 minute. Measure out 1 tablespoon of the browned-butter mixture and set aside. Add the squash mixture to the pan and continue to cook just until heated through, 3–5 minutes. Taste and adjust the seasonings.

Transfer to a warmed serving bowl, drizzle the reserved browned-butter mixture over the squash, and serve right away.

butternut squash,
1 small (about 1½ pounds)

firm but ripe pears such as anjou or bosc, 2

extra-virgin olive oil,
2 tablespoons, plus oil for greasing

sea salt and freshly ground pepper

unsalted butter,
2 tablespoons

fresh ginger, ½-inch piece, peeled and minced

fresh sage, 6 leaves, cut into thin ribbons

MAKES 4 SERVINGS

Unsmoked, but still highly flavored, Italian pancetta has a purer flavor than that of smoked bacon. When cooked together, the peppered meat echoes the peppery mustard greens while still letting the greens' natural pungency shine.

braised mustard greens with pancetta and lemon

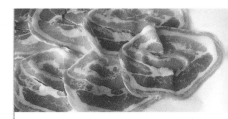

pancetta, 2 ounces, diced

unsalted butter,
1 tablespoon

garlic, 1 clove, minced

mustard greens, 2 bunches
(about 3 pounds total
weight), stemmed and
coarsely chopped

**sea salt and freshly
ground pepper**

low-sodium chicken broth,
1 cup

lemon, ½

MAKES 4 SERVINGS

In a frying pan over medium-high heat, sauté the pancetta until it is lightly browned and crisp, 4–5 minutes. Transfer the pancetta to a paper towel–lined plate to drain and set aside.

Pour out all but 1 tablespoon of the fat from the pan and reduce the heat to medium-low. Add the butter. When it has melted, add the garlic and sauté until fragrant, about 1 minute. Add the mustard greens and a generous pinch each of salt and pepper and cook, stirring occasionally, until the greens begin to wilt, 3–4 minutes. Add the broth and cook, stirring occasionally, until the greens are tender but still bright green and the liquid reduces to a glaze, 8–10 minutes.

Transfer the greens to a warmed serving dish. If there is cooking liquid left in the pan, simmer it until it is syrupy and reduces to about 1 tablespoon. Pour the liquid over the greens and toss to combine. Taste and adjust the seasonings, then squeeze the juice from the lemon half over the greens. Top with the crisp pancetta and serve right away.

Salty, pepper-flecked Italian pancetta both contrasts with and complements the peppery bite of mustard greens in this simple recipe. Braising the greens in chicken broth adds richness and dimension to the dish and further softens any harshness in the greens. A spritz of lemon juice freshens and harmonizes the flavors.

pan-grilled radicchio with italian-style salsa verde

Ruby-red radicchio is delightfully bitter. Grilling thick wedges of it caramelizes and sweetens the outer leaves. The salsa verde adds a contrasting color as well piquancy that brightens the winter chicory. When seasoning the salsa verde, be sure to taste it first since the anchovies and capers both have a measure of natural saltiness.

Remove and discard any blemished or discolored leaves from the radicchio heads, then cut each head into quarters. Arrange the quarters on a baking sheet, drizzle them lightly with oil, sprinkle lightly with salt and pepper, and toss to coat. Set aside.

Finely grate the zest from the lemon, then halve the fruit and squeeze the juice from one half into a small bowl. Set aside the remaining half.

In the bowl of a food processor, combine the lemon zest, garlic, horseradish, capers, and anchovies. Process until well chopped. Add the parsley and mint leaves, lemon juice, and 2 tablespoons of the oil. Pulse until the mixture forms a coarse purée. With the motor running, slowly pour in the remaining 6 tablespoons oil and process until smooth; it should have the consistency of pesto. Transfer the mixture to a bowl and taste and adjust the seasonings. If desired, add a bit more lemon juice.

Heat a ridged grill pan on the stove top over medium heat. When it is hot, add the radicchio quarters in a single layer and cook until they just begin to wilt and caramelize, 2–3 minutes per side. Transfer to a serving plate and drizzle with the salsa verde. Serve hot or at room temperature.

treviso radicchio, 4 heads

extra-virgin olive oil, 8 tablespoons, plus oil for drizzling

sea salt and freshly ground pepper

lemon, 1

garlic, 2 cloves, smashed

prepared horseradish, 1 teaspoon

capers, 2 tablespoons

oil-packed anchovy fillets, preferably italian, 2

fresh flat-leaf parsley, leaves from 1 bunch

fresh mint, leaves from ½ bunch

MAKES 4 SERVINGS

braised winter vegetables with coconut and red curry

canola oil, 2 teaspoons

garlic, 1 clove, minced

fresh ginger, ¼-inch slice, peeled and grated

red curry paste, 2 teaspoons

thai fish sauce, 1 teaspoon

sweet potato, 1 (about ½ pound), peeled and cut into ½-inch chunks

celery root, 1 (about ½ pound), peeled and cut into ½-inch chunks

unsweetened coconut milk, 3 cups

delicata squash, 1 (about ½ pound)

lime, 1

fresh cilantro, 8 sprigs

MAKES 4 SERVINGS

In a saucepan over medium heat, warm the oil. When the oil is hot, add the garlic and ginger and sauté until fragrant but not browned, about 1 minute. Add the curry paste and cook, stirring, for 1 minute. Add the fish sauce, sweet potato, and celery root and stir to combine. Reduce the heat to medium-low, pour in the coconut milk and cook, stirring occasionally, for 10 minutes. Add the squash and cook until the vegetables are just tender when pierced with a sharp knife but not falling apart, 12–15 minutes.

While the vegetables are cooking, finely grate the zest from the lime and cut the fruit into wedges. Stir the lime zest into the vegetables.

Divide the vegetables and braising liquid among warmed bowls, top each with 2 sprigs of cilantro and a lime wedge, and serve right away.

Coconut milk lends richness and exotic flavor to these creamy braised vegetables. Its slight sweetness echoes that of both the root vegetables and squash, while offsetting the spicy red curry paste, pungent Asian fish sauce, and bright lime and cilantro that season the broth.

Sweet, slightly nutty parsnips are often overshadowed by the more popular carrots and potatoes. But roasted and mixed with other nutty flavorings, like brown butter and toasted hazelnuts, they make an unexpectedly savory side dish.

parsnips and sweet potatoes with hazelnuts and brown butter

hazelnuts, 3 tablespoons, coarsely chopped

canola oil, 3 tablespoons

parsnips, 2 (about 1 pound total weight)

sweet potato, 1 (about 1 pound)

sea salt and freshly ground pepper

unsalted butter, 2 tablespoons

fresh thyme, 1 teaspoon minced

MAKES 4 SERVINGS

In a small, dry frying pan over medium-low heat, toast the hazelnuts until they turn a deep brown and are fragrant, 3–5 minutes. While the nuts are still warm, wrap them in a clean kitchen towel. Rub the nuts vigorously to remove the skins; it is fine if some bits of skin remain. Set aside.

Preheat the oven to 425°F. Drizzle 1½ tablespoons of the oil onto each of 2 rimmed baking sheets. Place the sheets in the oven to preheat while you prepare the vegetables.

Peel the parsnips and sweet potato, then cut them into pieces about ½ inch thick and 2–3 inches long. Remove the baking sheets from the oven and divide the vegetables between them. Sprinkle lightly with salt and pepper, toss the vegetables to coat them with the warm oil, and spread them out in a single layer. Roast until the undersides are nicely browned and crisp, 10–12 minutes. Turn each piece once or twice and roast until the vegetables are browned on all sides, 8–10 minutes longer.

In a small frying pan over medium heat, warm the butter, stirring occasionally, until it begins to turn brown and smell nutty, 3–4 minutes. Remove the pan from the heat and stir in the hazelnuts and thyme.

Transfer the roasted vegetables to a large bowl, drizzle with the browned butter mixture, and toss gently to coat. Taste and adjust the seasonings and serve right away.

Intensely nutty hazelnuts echo the taste of butter cooked until rich golden brown. The deep flavor of both the toasted nuts and brown butter pairs well with the earthy root vegetables, whose high level of natural sugars caramelize when roasted. Fragrant thyme leaves impart an herbal taste to the dish.

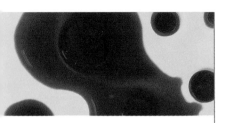

balsamic-braised red cabbage

Balsamic vinegar's honeyed, mildly tart quality stands in for harsher red wine vinegar in this new twist on a classic recipe. Green apples lend both sweetness and brightness, red wine adds depth, and a sprinkle of orange zest contributes freshness to this hearty side dish.

In a large frying pan over medium heat, warm the oil. When the oil is hot, add the onion and a pinch of salt and sauté until the onion is soft and translucent, 5–7 minutes. Add the honey and cook for 1 minute longer. Add the apple slices and vinegar, raise the heat to medium-high, and use a wooden spoon to scrape up any browned bits from the bottom of the pan. Bring the liquid to a boil, then add the wine and 1 cup water. Season with a generous pinch each of salt and pepper and return to a boil. Reduce the heat to medium-low and simmer until the liquid begins to reduce, about 10 minutes.

Add the cabbage and, using tongs, toss well to coat with the liquid in the pan. Cover the pan and cook the cabbage, stirring occasionally, until it begins to wilt, 25–30 minutes. Uncover and cook until the cabbage is tender and most of the liquid has evaporated, 25–30 minutes longer.

Taste and adjust the seasonings. Remove the pan from the heat and finely grate the zest from the orange over the cabbage (reserve the fruit for another use). Stir well to evenly distribute the zest, then transfer the cabbage to a warmed bowl, and serve right away.

extra-virgin olive oil, 3 tablespoons

yellow onion, 1, thinly sliced

sea salt and freshly ground pepper

honey, 1 tablespoon

tart green apple such as granny smith, 1, halved, cored, and thinly sliced

balsamic vinegar, ¼ cup

dry red wine such as merlot, 1 cup

red cabbage, 1 head (about 2 pounds), cored and cut into thin shreds

orange, 1

MAKES 4–6 SERVINGS

individual swiss chard gratins

unsalted butter,
3 tablespoons, plus
butter for greasing

fresh marjoram,
½ teaspoon minced

fresh thyme, ½ teaspoon
minced

**fresh bread crumbs (page
145),** ½ cup

**freshly grated parmesan
cheese,** 2 teaspoons

**sea salt and freshly
ground pepper**

swiss chard, 2 bunches

extra-virgin olive oil,
1 tablespoon

shallots, 2, minced

all-purpose flour,
1½ tablespoons

**whole milk and heavy
cream,** ½ cup each

freshly grated nutmeg,
pinch

**swiss gruyére or french
comté cheese,** 1½ ounces,
shredded

MAKES 4 SERVINGS

Preheat the oven to 400°F. Butter four ¾-cup ramekins.

In a bowl, combine the marjoram, thyme, bread crumbs, Parmesan, and
a pinch each of salt and pepper and toss well. In a small saucepan, melt
1 tablespoon of the butter, then drizzle it over the crumb mixture and stir
to mix well. Set aside.

Strip the chard leaves from the stems and tear the leaves into bite-sized
pieces. Cut off and discard the tough bottoms of the stems, then finely
mince enough of the remaining stems to measure ½ cup.

In a large frying pan over medium heat, warm the oil. When the oil is hot, add
the shallots, chard stems, and a pinch of salt and sauté until the shallots
are soft and translucent, 5–6 minutes. Reduce the heat to medium-low,
add the chard leaves, and stir to combine. Cover the pan and cook until
the leaves just begin to wilt, 2–3 minutes. Uncover, raise the heat to
medium, and cook until the leaves are wilted and the liquid evaporates,
2–3 minutes longer. Remove from the heat.

In a small saucepan over medium heat, melt the remaining 2 tablespoons
butter. Add the flour and cook, whisking constantly, for about 1 minute.
Whisk in the milk and cream, bring to a boil, and cook until smooth. Reduce
the heat to medium-low and cook until thickened, 1–2 minutes. Remove
from the heat, and add the nutmeg and a pinch each of salt and pepper.
Stir in the Gruyère until smooth, then stir in the chard mixture. Divide
the mixture evenly among the prepared ramekins and sprinkle the herbed
bread crumbs over the top. Bake until the crumbs are lightly browned
and the chard is warm and bubbling, 15–17 minutes.

Remove from the oven and let rest for 5 minutes. Serve right away.

*High-quality Gruyère
cheese has a creamy,
nutty taste and it melts
beautifully. Here, it gilds
a rich white sauce that
is mixed with mildly
bitter swiss chard, then
baked into individual
casseroles. A crisp topping
of buttery, Parmesan-
flecked bread crumbs adds
an appealing crunch.*

Aromatic infused oils offer a simple way to add high-impact flavor to your cooking and add bold bright accents to winter's hearty vegetables. Here, spicy chile oil gives mild, fresh bok choy a surprising kick in a simple stir fry.

wok-seared baby bok choy with chile oil and garlic

sesame seeds,
1 tablespoon

baby bok choy, 4 heads
(about 1 pound total
weight)

canola oil,
1½ tablespoons

garlic, 3 cloves, thinly sliced

red pepper flakes,
½ teaspoon

sea salt

low-sodium chicken broth,
¼ cup

asian chile oil, 2 teaspoons

MAKES 4 SERVINGS

In a dry pan over medium heat, toast the sesame seeds until golden brown and fragrant, 4–5 minutes. Pour onto a plate to cool and set aside.

Cut off the tough base from each head of bok choy. Separate the heads into individual stalks by snapping the stalks away from their cores.

In a wok or a large frying pan over medium-high heat, warm the canola oil. When it is hot and shimmering in the pan, add the garlic and red pepper flakes and cook, tossing and stirring constantly, until fragrant but not browned, 20–30 seconds. Add the bok choy and a pinch of salt and cook, tossing and stirring, until the bok choy just begins to wilt, 1–2 minutes. Add the broth and cook, stirring occasionally, until the bok choy is just tender and the broth evaporates, 1–2 minutes. Add the chile oil, stir well to coat the bok choy, and remove from the heat.

Stir in the toasted sesame seeds, transfer the mixture to a warmed serving bowl, and serve right away.

Spicy red chile oil delivers its pure bold flavor to a quick stir-fry of baby bok choy. Accented by nutty sesame seeds, assertive garlic, and spicy red pepper flakes, this side dish perks up a midwinter meal.

fundamentals

The following basic recipes are either called for in this book or are hearty grain-and pasta-based sides that you can pair with vegetable dishes for complete meals. Also in these pages are some key techniques for dicing and chopping vegetables, working with a variety of herbs, and tips for setting up your gas or charcoal grill, all of which will help you make dishes that are both beautiful and delicious.

crème fraîche

1 cup heavy cream

1 tablespoon buttermilk

In a small saucepan over medium-low heat, combine the cream and buttermilk. Heat just until the mixture is lukewarm (do not allow the mixture to simmer). Transfer the mixture to a bowl, cover, and let stand at room temperature until thickened, at least 8 hours and up to 48 hours. Refrigerate until well chilled before using. Makes about 1 cup.

cooked white rice

1 cup long-grain white rice

1½ cups water

Place the rice in a fine-mesh sieve and rinse under cold running water until the water runs clear. Transfer the rice to a heavy saucepan and add the water. Cover the pan, place it over high heat, and bring to a boil. Reduce the heat to low and simmer, undisturbed, for about 20 minutes. Remove from the heat and let stand, covered, for 5 minutes. Fluff

the rice with a fork and serve right away. Makes 4–6 servings.

rice pilaf

1 tablespoon unsalted butter

¼ cup chopped onion

1 cup long-grain white rice

1½ cups low-sodium chicken broth

¼ teaspoon salt

1 tablespoon toasted slivered almonds

Melt the butter in a large saucepan over low heat. Add the onion and cook, stirring occasionally, until golden, about 8 minutes. Stir the rice into the saucepan and cook for about 3 minutes. Stir in the chicken broth and salt and bring to a boil.

Cover the saucepan and simmer until the liquid is absorbed and the rice is tender, about 15 minutes. Let stand, covered, for 5 minutes.

Fluff the rice with a fork, gently stir in the toasted almonds, and serve right away. Makes 4–6 servings.

basic couscous

2 cups water

½ teaspoon salt

2 cups instant couscous

In a small saucepan over high heat, combine the water and salt and bring to a boil. Stirring constantly, pour in the couscous. Remove from the heat, cover, and let stand for about 5 minutes. Transfer to a bowl, fluff with a fork, and serve right away. Makes 4 servings.

polenta

5 cups water

1½ cups fine-ground polenta

½ teaspoon salt

In a large saucepan over medium-high heat, bring the water to a boil. Whisking constantly, add the polenta in a slow stream. Stir in the salt, reduce the heat to medium-low, and continue to cook, stirring constantly, until the polenta thickens and pulls away from the sides of the pan, about 20 minutes. Serve right away. Makes 4–6 servings.

preparing vegetables

Washing is the first step to preparing most vegetables. Even if you're peeling a vegetable, it is important to wash it first, so that the dirt or chemicals don't transfer from the peeler to the flesh of the vegetable. Wash vegetables under cold running water, then set them out to dry or use a clean kitchen towel to dry them. Mushrooms soak up water and should not be rinsed. Use a soft brush or a damp cloth to wipe them clean.

shelling beans and peas

1 Split the pod Have ready a small bowl. Working with 1 pod at a time, pinch the tip at each end to begin splitting the pod. Squeeze the pod, pressing your thumb against the seam to coax it open.

2 Pop out the beans or peas Sweep your thumb down along the inside of the pod to pop out the beans or peas and let them fall into the bowl. Discard the pod. Repeat with the remaining pods.

trimming broccoli

1 Cut off the stalk Using a chef's knife, cut off the stalk right up to where it joins with the crown.

2 Cut the broccoli into florets Using a paring knife, cut the broccoli crown into individual florets, each about 1 inch long. If the florets seem too big when cut from the stalk, cut them gently through the stem end so as not to damage the crown.

trimming cauliflower

1 Remove the core and leaves Using a chef's knife, cut the head of cauliflower in half vertically to reveal the core. Use a paring knife to cut out the inner core and trim away any green leaves.

2 Cut the cauliflower into florets Cut the cauliflower head into florets, each about 1 inch long. If the stems of the florets seem tough, use the paring knife to peel them.

working with mushrooms

1 Brush or wipe away the dirt Using a mushroom brush or damp cloth, gently brush or wipe away any dirt from the mushrooms.

2 Trim the stems Using a paring knife, trim a thin slice from the base of the stem of each mushroom and discard. If slicing the mushroom caps, cut off the whole stem.

working with onions

1 Halve and peel the onion Slice the stem end off of the onion, halve it lengthwise from the stem to root end, then peel it.

2 Make a series of vertical cuts Put an onion half flat side down on a cutting board, holding it with your fingertips safely curled under and away from the blade, and, with the knife tip pointed toward the root end, make a series of parallel vertical cuts at right angles to the cutting board. Do not cut all the way through the root end.

3 Make a series of horizontal cuts Turn the knife so that it is parallel with the cutting board and perpendicular to the first series of cuts, and make another series of horizontal cuts in the onion half, again not cutting through the root end.

4 Dice the onion Slice the onion across the 2 cuts made in steps 2 and 3.

finely diced For a finer dice, follow steps 1–4 for dicing onions, making all of the cuts closer together.

thinly slicing To thinly slice an onion, complete step 1, then put it flat-side down on a cutting board. With your fingers safely curled under and away from the blade, cut the onion into thin slices.

cutting up root vegetables

1 Peel the vegetable Using a vegetable peeler, preferably one with a swivel blade, remove the peel from the vegetable.

2 Cut the vegetable in half Trim off both ends of the vegetable, then cut it in half lengthwise. Place the vegetable, flat side down, on the cutting board.

3 Cut the halves into pieces Many recipes call for cutting vegetables into 1–2-inch chunks or pieces. You can achieve this by creating both lengthwise and crosswise cuts so that you have square-shaped pieces. Or, you can cut small, slender vegetables, like carrots and parsnips, lengthwise for a different effect. For mixed vegetable dishes, it is important that all of the pieces are the same size so they will cook evenly.

dicing tomatoes

1 Cut vertical slices Using a chef's knife, make a shallow circular cut to remove the tomato core, then cut the tomato in half through the core. Place each half cut side down and make a series of slices, 1/8–1/4 inch apart.

2 Cut the slices into strips Stack 2 or 3 of the tomato slices at a time on their sides. Make a second series of slices, 1/8–1/4 inch apart, perpendicular to the first. You will end up wth strips.

3 Cut the strips into dice Line up the strips and cut crosswise into 1/8- to 1/4-inch dice. Repeat steps 1–3 with the remaining tomato halves.

4 Transfer the dice Use the flat side of the chef's knife to scoop up the pieces and transfer them to a bowl.

working with winter squash

1 Halve the squash If cutting the squash into chunks, first peel it using a vegetable peeler. Using a large chef's knife, cut the neck off the squash, if necessary. Cut both sections in half lengthwise.

2 Scoop out the seeds Using a metal spoon, scoop out and discard the seeds and any strings from each half as needed.

3 Slice or dice the squash With the flat, hollowed out side of the squash facing down on the cutting board, cut the squash crosswise into slices. If directed, cut the squash slices crosswise into chunks.

working with herbs

chopping marjoram, chervil, parsley, mint, cilantro, tarragon, or sage Pull off the leaves from the stems; discard the stems or save them for stock. Gather the leaves on a cutting board and then rock a chef's knife back and forth over the leaves until chopped into large pieces (coarsely chop). Regather the leaves and rock the blade over them until chopped into pieces as small as possible (mince).

cutting mint, basil, or sage into ribbons Pull off the leaves from the stems; discard the stems and any discolored or badly ripped leaves. Stack 5 or 6 herb leaves on top of one another, then roll the stack lengthwise into a tight cylinder. Using a chef's knife, cut the leaves crosswise into narrow ribbons.

chopping thyme and rosemary Gently run your thumb and index finger down the stems to remove the leaves. Gather the leaves on a cutting board. Rock a chef's knife back and forth over the leaves to chop into large pieces (coarsely chop). Regather the leaves and rock the blade over them until they are chopped into pieces as small as possible (mince).

snipping chives Gather the chives into a small bundle and place on a cutting board. Using a very sharp chef's knife, cut the chives crosswise into small pieces. Alternatively, hold the bundle in one hand and use kitchen scissors to snip the chives into small pieces.

working with shallots

1 Separate the cloves Sometimes you'll find plump, individual bronze-skinned shallots; other times they resemble garlic heads, with 2 or more cloves attached to one another. Separate the cloves, if necessary.

2 Halve the shallot Using a paring knife or chef's knife, cut the shallot in half lengthwise through the root end.

3 Peel and trim the shallot Using the knife, pick up the edge of the shallot's papery skin and pull it away. Trim each end neatly, but leave some of the root intact to help hold the shallot half together.

4 Cut the shallot half lengthwise Put the flat side of the shallot half on the cutting board and make a series of lengthwise cuts. Do not cut all the way through the root end; it helps hold the shallot layers together.

5 Cut the shallot half horizontally Turn the knife blade parallel to the cutting board and make a series of thin horizontal cuts through the shallot half, stopping just short of the root end.

6 *Cut the shallot half crosswise* Cut the shallot half crosswise to make dice. Dicing a shallot in this methodical way yields uniform pieces that will cook evenly.

thinly slicing To thinly slice a shallot, follow steps 1–3. Place the flat side of the shallot half on the cutting board. Using a paring knife or a chef's knife, cut the shallot crosswise into thin slices.

working with garlic

1 *Loosen the garlic peel* Using the flat side of a chef's knife, firmly press against the clove. If you plan to mince the garlic, it's fine to smash it. If you are slicing it, use light pressure to keep the garlic clove intact.

2 *Peel and halve the clove* The pressure from the knife will cause the garlic peel to split; pull it off and discard. Cut the garlic clove in half lengthwise through the root end.

3 *Cut the garlic half into slices* One at a time, use the knife to cut the garlic clove halves into very thin slices crosswise or lengthwise. Use the slices as is or chop them.

4 *Chop the garlic* Hold the knife handle with one hand; rest the fingertips of your other hand on the knife tip. Rock the knife blade back and forth over the sliced garlic until evenly chopped. Use as is or mince the garlic.

5 *Mince the garlic* Gather the chopped garlic in a compact pile on the board. Clean the garlic bits off the knife and add them to the pile. Continue to chop, rocking the blade back and forth, until the garlic pieces are very fine, or minced.

working with ginger

1 *Peel the ginger* Using a paring knife, vegetable peeler, or the tip of a spoon, peel away the papery brown skin from the ginger.

2 *Cut the ginger into disks* Grip the ginger with one hand and, using a utility knife, paring knife, or chef's knife, cut the ginger into disks.

3 *Cut the disks into thin strips* Stack the disks on top of each other, a few at a time, and cut the disks into strips.

4 *Chop the strips* Line up the strips and cut them crosswise to coarsely chop. Continue to chop, rocking the blade back and forth, until the pieces are very fine, or minced.

working with chiles

1 *Quarter the chile lengthwise* Using a paring knife, cut the chile into halves lengthwise, then into quarters.

2 *Remove the seeds and ribs* Using a paring knife, cut away the stem, seeds, and ribs from each chile quarter.

3 *Slice the quarters into strips* Place the quarters, cut side up, on the cutting board. Cut into narrow strips about ⅛ inch wide.

4 *Dice and mince the strips* Line up the chile strips and cut them crosswise at ⅛-inch intervals. Rest the fingertips of one hand on the top of the knife and rock the blade back and forth over the pieces to mince them.

pitting olives

1 *Pound the olives* Place the olives in a locking plastic bag, force out the air, and seal closed. Using a meat pounder or a rolling pin, gently pound the olives to loosen the pits.

2 *Remove the pits* Remove the crushed olives from the bag and separate the pits from the olive flesh with your fingers. Use a paring knife to cut the flesh from the pits of any stubborn olives.

making fresh bread crumbs

Trim off the crusts from a baguette or other country-style bread and tear the slices into large pieces. Process in a food processor until the bread forms crumbs the size you want. Alternatively, to prepare the crumbs by hand, use the crust as a handle and grate the bread on the large holes of a box grater-shredder.

working with citrus

1 *Wash and grate the citrus* Wash the fruit well. Use a rasp grater, such as a Microplane grater, or the finest rasps of a box grater-shredder to remove the colored part of the peel, not the bitter white pith.

2 *Clean off the grater* Don't forget to scrape all the zest from the back of the grater, where some of it naturally gathers.

3 *Halve the citrus* First press and roll the citrus fruit firmly against the counter to soften the fruit. Then, using a chef's knife, cut the fruit in half crosswise.

4 *Juice the citrus* If juicing by hand, use a citrus reamer to pierce the membranes as you squeeze. Catch the juice in a bowl. Strain the juice into another bowl, if necessary, to remove the seeds before using.

direct-heat grilling

charcoal grill Using long-handled tongs, arrange ignited coals into 3 heat zones: one 2 or 3 layers deep in one-third of the fire bed, another that's 1 or 2 layers deep in another third of the fire bed, leaving the final third of the fire bed free of coals. When the coals are covered with a layer of white ash, place the food on the grill grate directly over the first layer of coals, which should be the hottest. Move the food to another third of the grill if the heat seems too high, the food appears to be cooking too fast, or if flare-ups occur.

gas grill Turn on all the heat elements as high as they will go. Close the grill cover and let the grill heat for 10–20 minutes before using. When you're ready to cook, turn one of the heat elements off. Place the food on the grill grate directly over the hottest part of the grill. Turn down the heat as needed to adjust the grill temperature, or move the food to the cool zone if flare-ups occur.

choosing vegetables

The recipes in this book encourage you to be inspired by the bounty of seasonal produce available at local farmers' markets, roadside farm stands, and grocery stores. The fresher the vegetables you start with, the more flavorful the whole dish will be. As they sit in the market, vegetables will lose moisture, crunch, and overall flavor. High-quality vegetables should look plump, moist, and unwrinkled and should be heavy for their size. One benefit of patronizing a farmers' market is that you can ask the farmer when the vegetables were picked and sometimes they offer samples for you to taste. That way, you can judge the freshness for yourself.

Some vegetables, such as corn on the cob, tomatoes, and artichokes, begin to lose their freshness as soon as they are harvested. Others, such as hard-shelled winter squashes, potatoes, and carrots, can be stored for relatively long periods of time.

buying organically

The benefit of buying organic produce is that it hasn't been grown in soil that is chemically treated and the vegetables and fruits themselves haven't been sprayed with pesticides. Although organic produce has a shorter shelf life, this means they are often fresher when found on supermarket shelves. One drawback is that organically grown vegetables and fruits can be more expensive than their conventionally grown counterparts. However, some vegetables and fruits retain more chemicals than others. A more budget-friendly way to incorporate organic food into your lifestyle is to sensibly mix and match organically and conventionally grown produce.

Produce that retains a lot of the chemicals it is grown with include: apples, apricots, bell peppers, celery, cherries, spinach, strawberries, peaches, pears, potatoes, raspberries, bell peppers, and cucumbers. When shopping for these fruits and vegetables, it might be worth it to splurge for the organic varieties.

Some fruits and vegetables are less likely to absorb the chemicals they are grown with, so it's not as important to buy the organically grown varieties; these include: asparagus, avocados, bananas, broccoli, cauliflower, corn, kiwi, mangos, onions, papayas, pineapples, and sweet peas.

You can usually find less expensive organic produce at farmers' markets because it has been grown locally. Organic foods found in supermarkets are sometimes imported and can be twice as expensive. To be sure the foods are truly organic, look for a label that says "100 percent organic."

storing produce

Leafy greens and herbs do not keep well, so it's best to store them in the vegetable crisper of your refrigerator for only a few days. Greens are best when they are cold, crisp, and dry, so wash them a few hours before you plan to use them, then dry in a salad spinner, wrap in a towel, and store in the crisper drawer until ready to serve. You can also store leafy herbs upright in a drinking glass with water for several hours.

Cabbages and root vegetables such as turnips and parsnips are good keepers. These wintertime vegetables can hold onto their flavor, texture, and nutrients for several weeks after harvesting. Store them in the vegetable crisper of the refrigerator for up to 2 weeks. Sturdy summer vegetables, such as zucchini and eggplant, also do well in the crisper, but for a shorter time.

Onions, shallots, and garlic can all be stored at room temperature and usually stay fresh for about 3 weeks. Keep these vegetables in a cool place, preferably in a basket where the air can circulate. Potatoes must be stored in a dark pantry or cupboard, as light will cause them to turn green and bitter.

seasoning vegetables

A bit of butter or olive oil and a pinch or two of salt and freshly ground pepper help any fresh vegetable taste great, but adding a few more elements like citrus juice and zest, fresh herbs, and bold condiments can significantly elevate your vegetable dishes.

salt Salt helps draw out and build flavors. If you start salting at the very beginning of the cooking, whether this means salting the water to boil potatoes, or to season a marinade, once you get to the final step, you may need to add very little salt to sharpen the flavors. Also, everyone has a different tolerance for salt and pepper, so don't only rely on a recipe; it's better to taste and season to suit your own tastes.

butter and oil Butter is delicious mixed with vegetables, but it can burn at high temperatures, so oil is better for sautéing. Olive oil is a delicious and health-smart choice. For a fruity and flavorful olive oil for cooking, look for moderately priced bottles labeled extra-virgin. For a lighter cooking oil, turn to pure olive oil or a vegetable oil, such as canola. Use a more expensive extra-virgin olive oil for drizzling over a finished dish. Asian sesame oil is also a good finishing oil.

acidic ingredients Fresh lemon or lime juice and vinegars of all types add a touch of sharpness to a dish. Sometimes a few drops are all that are needed to heighten the flavors. Most acidic ingredients also contribute their own distinctive flavors—the brightness of lemon, the depth of an oak-aged red wine vinegar—to a dish.

fresh herbs The floral complexity of fresh herbs disappears when they are dried, so buying fresh is usually better. While woody herbs are often added towards the beginning of cooking, leafy herbs are better saved for stirring in during the final cooking stages or for sprinkling on top of the finished dish; when heated, they lose their fresh, bright taste.

international pantry This book draws on flavors from around the world in the form of condiments (harissa and wasabi), spices (Indian curry powder and Mexican oregano) and oils (extra-virgin olive oil and Asian sesame oil). Most of these ingredients can be found at grocery stores or specialty food stores and many have long shelf lives, so once you buy them you will have them on hand to use in recipes or just to spice up basic steamed or roasted vegetables.

serving vegetables

The recipes in this book are designed to serve 4 people as a side dish. Many of these vegetable dishes would be delicious paired with meats cooked to suit the season, such as pan-fried lamb chops in the spring, grilled steaks in the summer, roast chicken in the fall, or a braised meat in the winter.

You can also serve the dishes in this book alongside polenta, rice, couscous, or pasta (see page 142) to make delicious vegetarian main-course meals.

seasonal ingredients

All produce has a peak season----sometimes just one month----where the taste is as good as it gets. Some vegetables, like spinach, arugula, potatoes, artichokes, bok choy, beets, and onions are also delicious towards the beginning or end of their growing seasons (see the open dots at right marking transitional seasons for some fruits and vegetables).

INGREDIENTS	SPRING	SUMMER	FALL	WINTER
apples			●	○
artichokes	●		●	
arugula	●	●	●	
asparagus	●			
beans, fava	●			
beans, shelling		●	●	
beans, green		●		
beets		●	●	
bok choy	●		●	●
broccoli		●	●	●
broccoli rabe		●	●	●
brussels sprouts			●	●
cabbage		●	●	○
carrots	●	○	●	●
cauliflower		●	●	●
celery root			●	○
chard	●	●	●	●
chiles		●	●	
citrus fruits	●			●
corn		●	○	
cucumber		●		

INGREDIENTS	SPRING	SUMMER	FALL	WINTER
eggplant		●	○	
kale	○		●	●
leeks	○	○	●	●
mushrooms, cultivated	●	●	●	●
mushrooms, wild			●	●
mustard greens	●	○		
okra		●	●	
onions, assorted		○	●	○
onions, green	●	●	○	
onions, vidalia	●			
parsnips	○		●	●
pears			●	●
peas	●	○		
potatoes	○	●	●	●
radicchio		●	●	●
radishes	●	●	●	
spinach	○	●	●	●
squash, summer		●	○	
squash, winter			●	●
tomatoes		●	○	
turnips	○		●	●

glossary

anchovies, oil-packed Harvested in waters worldwide, these small silver fish, popular in the Mediterranean, are often grilled. Most anchovies are preserved in salt or oil and sold packed in tins or jars.

artichokes, globe These flower buds from a plant of the sizable thistle family have a mild, nutty flavor. They are best in early spring, but have a secondary season in the fall. Look for artichokes that are heavy for their size.

arugula The leaves of this dark green plant, also called rocket, resemble deeply notched, elongated oak leaves. They have a nutty, tangy, and slightly peppery flavor. Mature arugula is often more pungent than mild, tender baby arugula.

asparagus Asparagus is one of the favorite springtime vegetables. Before cooking, check for a tough, fibrous inedible portion at the base of each spear. Cut off the dry, coarse-looking base or simply break off the tough end of each spear by bending it gently until it snaps. If the skin seems thick and tough, use a vegetable peeler or paring knife to peel the stalk to within about 2 inches of the tip.

beans There is a wide variety of beans in markets today. They are sold fresh, dried, canned, and even frozen.

black Black beans, sometime called turtle beans, have a firm, dense cooked texture and a very mild, slightly sweet flavor. They are sold both dried and in cans.

cannellini These ivory-colored beans possess a creamy, fluffy texture when cooked. White kidney beans or Great Northern beans may be substituted if dried or canned cannellini beans are unavailable.

fava Also called broad beans, this springtime bean has an earthy, slightly bitter flavor. The edible portion must be removed from the large outer pod, and then each bean must be slipped out of its tough skin.

green Green beans, also called string beans, are eaten whole and have a mild taste with fresh grassy overtones. When buying, look for vividly colored blemish-free pods with no signs of shriveling.

shell Shell beans are fresh beans that must be shelled, or removed from the pod, before cooking. Red-speckled cranberry beans, sometimes called borlotti beans, are one example

bok choy, baby Whether the white-stalked regular bok choy or jade-colored Shanghai variety, any type of bok choy that is harvested while the head is small can be called baby bok choy. Most well-stocked grocery stores sell at least one variety, but for the best selection, visit a Chinese market.

bread, country-style This general category includes any rustic, full-bodied, usually free-form yeast bread. French bread and baguettes are included in this group and are good choices for making hearty-textured bread cubes and crumbs.

broccoli rabe Also known as broccoli raab, rape, and rapini, this bright green vegetable resembles broccoli, but has slender stalks, small florets, and lots of frilly leaves. Its flavor is assertively bitter.

broth Any commercially made and packaged stock made by cooking vegetables, chicken, beef, or fish in water is called a broth. It can be a convenient substitute for homemade stock, but it tends to be more salty. Seek out low-sodium and low-fat broths, which will allow you more control in seasoning.

brown sugar, light Rich in flavor, brown sugar is granulated sugar mixed with molasses. It has a soft, moist texture. Light brown sugar is lighter in color and flavor than the dark brown variety.

Brussels sprouts A member of the cabbage family, Brussels sprouts grow on long stalks as tightly closed heads that resemble tiny cabbages. Select those that are heavy for their size with leaves tightly clinging to their heads. Small heads, about 1 inch in diameter, are usually preferable to large ones.

butter, unsalted Unsalted butter has not been seasoned with salt during its manufacture, giving the cook or baker full control over the amount of salt that is added to a recipe. It is sometimes called sweet butter, though sweet butter is also sold salted.

cabbage In grocery stores and farmers' markets, there are several cabbage varieties beyond the standard green cabbage. These are the types called for in this book.

Napa Also called Chinese cabbage or celery cabbage, this elongated variety has wrinkly, light yellow-green leaves and wide, flat, pearly white stalks.

red Red cabbage resembles green cabbage, but with a purple-red color. When buying, look for heads that have tightly packed leaves and feel heavy for their size.

capers Flower buds from a shrub native to the Mediterranean, capers are usually sold pickled in a vinegar brine. Those labeled "nonpareils," from the south of France, are the smallest and considered the best.

cayenne pepper A very hot red pepper made from ground dried cayenne chiles, cayenne is used sparingly to add heat or to heighten flavor. Because different blends vary in heat, and because only a little is needed, always begin with a very small amount and add more to taste in pinches.

celery root Also known as celeriac, celery root is a knobby, round winter vegetable that contributes a subtle celery flavor to purées when cooked and a crisp crunch to salads when used raw.

cheese Whether sprinkled over a finished dish or mixed into a stuffing to bind it, cheese plays an important role in many vegetable recipes. For the best flavor, shred or grate cheese just before use.

feta A white, crumbly sheep's or cow's milk cheese that is cured in brine, feta is a traditional Greek cheese, though it is now made in many countries, including the United States and France. It has a salty, tangy flavor.

fontina A rich, semifirm cow's milk cheese with an earthy, mild flavor, Italian fontina hails from Italy's Piedmont region. Non-Italian versions of the cheese are lacking in flavor, but all types are excellent for melting.

goat Also called *chèvre*, this pure white cheese is made from goat's milk. It has a soft texture and a pleasantly tangy, slightly salty flavor. Do not use the harder, aged goat cheese in a recipe calling for fresh.

Gruyère A firm, nutty-tasting cow's milk cheese, Gruyère is a Swiss cheese named for the alpine region in which it originated. It is also produced in France, where it is called Gruyère de Comté, or simply Comté. Both types have smooth melting qualities.

Parmesan Parmesan cheese is a firm, aged, salty cheese made from cow's milk. True Parmesan comes from the Emilia-Romagna region of northern Italy and is referred to by its trademarked name, *Parmigiano-Reggiano*. Rich and complex in flavor and often with a pleasant granular texture, this savory cheese is best when grated only as needed just before use in a recipe or at the table.

pecorino romano This Italian cheese made from sheep's milk has a sharp, salty flavor and a hard texture suitable for shaving or grating. Many domestically produced pecorino cheeses are made from cow's milk and have less flavor than the authentic version.

chestnuts, steamed Fresh chestnuts are always sold in their smooth mahogany-colored shells. They are very labor-intensive to cook and peel for use as an ingredient in a dish. Fortunately, steamed and shelled chestnuts are sold in jars in some grocery stores and specialty food stores, especially in the fall and winter. Chestnuts have a mild sweetness and meaty, starchy texture.

chiles When buying fresh chiles, seek out plump, firm, unblemished specimens. Use caution when handling fresh or dried chiles, as their heat is easily transferred to the skin.

chipotle, in adobo Chipotle chiles are ripe red jalapeños that have been dried and smoked. To make chipotle chiles in adobo, they are packed in a vinegary seasoned tomato sauce. Canned chipotle chiles in adobo are sold in most supermarkets.

jalapeño This bright green chile, averaging about 2 inches in length, ranges from hot to very hot and is one of the the most widely used chiles in the United States.

poblano Deep green with broad shoulders and a tapered body, a poblano chile is about 5 inches long. It is only mildly hot and has a green, earthy flavor.

coconut milk, unsweetened Sold in cans, coconut milk is made by processing grated coconut and water. Before use, shake the can to mix the cream that settles on the top with the liquid on the bottom.

crème fraîche In France, crème fraîche is unpasteurized cream thickened by bacteria that is naturally present in the cream. More commonly, though, it is cream thickened by a bacteria that is added, yielding a soft, spreadable consistency and a tangy flavor.

cucumber, English Slender, dark green English cucumbers, also called hothouse cucumbers, have thin skins and very few seeds. They are often sold shrink-wrapped besides regular cucumbers.

curry powder, Madras Curry powder is a conveniece product meant to simplify

the daily chore of blending spices for Indian cooks. It is a complex mixture of ground chiles, spices, seeds, and herbs. Madras curry has more heat than regular curry powders.

eggplant This versatile vegetable comes in many sizes and colors. There are two types used in recipes in this book.

Asian Slender, narrow Asian eggplants have very few seeds and are tender and mild in flavor. Deep purple Japanese eggplants are the most common, but lavender colored Chinese eggplants are available too.

globe This is the familiar eggplant variety. Large, purplish black, and bulbous globe eggplants are in grocery stores everywhere.

fish sauce Made from salted and fermented fish, this is a thin, clear liquid that ranges in color from amber to dark brown. In Southeast Asian cooking, it is used both as a cooking ingredient and as a seasoning at the table.

ham, Black Forest Traditionally, this ham is made in Germany according to strict guidelines. It is carefully seasoned, cured, and then smoked. The Black Forest ham that is widely available in this country is a smoked ham with a dark exterior made to look like the traditional version.

harissa This fiery North African spice paste is used both as a seasoning and as a condiment.

It is made with chiles, spices, garlic, and olive oil and is sold in tubes, cans, or jars in well-stocked grocery stores and Middle Eastern markets.

herbs Herbs enliven vegetable dishes with their perfume and distinct flavors. Most are best when used fresh, but some hearty herbs can be used dried. Many herbs have become commonplace; the more unusual ones used in this book are discussed below.

bay leaves The green-gray leaves of the laurel tree, bay leaves have a savory herbal fragrance. At one time, dried bay was the only type available, but fresh bay leaves, which have a more delicate and complex flavor than dried, have become increasingly available.

chervil, fresh A springtime herb with green leaves that resemble delicate parsley leaves, chervil is best when used fresh. It has a mild flavor reminiscent of parsley and anise.

chives Long, thin, and dark green, chives are a member of the onion family. They lend a mild onion-like flavor to dishes. Because of their color and shape, they are often used as a garnish.

Marjoram, fresh This herb has a flavor similar to its relative, oregano, but is much more delicate and has floral, minty hints.

Mexican oregano, dried This herb is unrelated to the oregano that flavors

Mediterranean foods. It has an herbal quality with hints of citrus that complement the foods with Mexican and Southwestern flavors. It is sold in Mexican grocery stores.

Sage, fresh Fuzzy sage leaves are grey-green and highly aromatic. The earthy taste of sage is often used to season meats and poultry, but it also works well in vegetable dishes with robust flavors.

Tarragon, fresh This mildly sweet herb has long, narrow, deep green leaves and a flavor reminiscent of anise. Use caution when adding tarragon, as its relatively strong flavor can overpower more delicate ingredients.

horseradish, prepared Horseradish is a gnarled root with a spicy flavor that perks up sauces and side dishes. It can be found fresh, but is more commonly sold bottled as prepared horseradish, already grated and mixed with vinegar or beet juice. Look for prepared horseradish in the refrigerated section of grocery stores.

kale, black Also known as black cabbage or *cavolo nero*, black kale is a dark, sturdy, leafy green very similar to dinosaur kale. If black kale is not available, dinosaur or regular kale is a fine substitute.

maple syrup, pure Maple syrup is made by boiling down the sap of the sugar maple tree to an amber-colored syrup. The syrup is graded according to color, from "Fancy" and Grade A which are both light in color and delicate in taste, to Grade B which is darker in color and more robust in taste. Grade B is generally only used in cooking and baking, not as a condiment.

mirin An important ingredient in Japanese cooking, mirin is a sweet cooking wine made by fermenting glutinous rice and sugar. The pale gold and syrupy wine adds a rich flavor and translucent sheen to sauces, dressings, and simmered dishes.

miso, white A staple of the Japanese kitchen, miso is a fermented paste of soybeans and grain. Relatively mild-tasting white miso, or *shiro-miso*, is one of the more common varieties. Look for white miso in the refrigerator case of well-stocked grocery or natural foods stores, or in Japanese markets.

mustard greens The dark green leaves of the mustard plant, mustard greens have a pungent, peppery bite. When shopping, choose greens with vibrant color and fresh, perky leaves.

okra A slender, grayish green, ridged pod that contains numerous seeds, okra is popular in the American South. It has a mild flavor similar to that of green beans and a viscous quality that thickens stews such as gumbo.

oils There is a wide variety of oils available to cooks today. Some are best used for high-heat cooking, some for drizzling over a finished dish as a flavor accent.

Asian chile This bottled oil, available in Asian markets and many supermarkets, has hot red chiles steeped in it; the chiles give the oil a red color and a searing heat.

Asian sesame A dark amber oil pressed from toasted white sesame seeds, Asian sesame oil has a distinctive nutty aroma and taste. Unlike other oils used for cooking, sesame oil is added in small amounts as a flavoring agent to marinades and dressings or to soups and braised or stir-fried dishes during the final minutes of cooking.

canola This neutral-tasting oil is pressed from rapeseed, a relative of the mustard plant. High in monounsaturated fat, it is good for general cooking.

extra-virgin olive The first cold pressing of olives yields extra-virgin olive oil, the variety that is the lowest in acid and the purest, with a full flavor that reflects where the olives were grown. This oil is best saved for drizzling on finished dishes.

Walnut Pressed from walnut meats, walnut oil has a rich, nutty flavor and fragrance. It is not used for cooking because its flavor is lost when heated; it is often used in salad dressings or for drizzling onto finished dishes.

olives, kalamata A popular olive variety from Greece, the Kalamata is almond shaped, purplish black, rich, and meaty. The olives are brine cured and then packed in oil or vinegar. They are sold in most supermarkets.

oyster sauce This thick, concentrated dark brown sauce made with dried oysters and soy sauce has a savory-sweet flavor. It is used as an ingredient and sometimes as a condiment in Asian, particularly Chinese, cooking. It is sold in most supermarkets and in Asian grocery stores.

pancetta Pancetta is unsmoked Italian bacon. To make it, pork belly is salted and seasoned with black pepper and other spices before it is rolled into a cylinder and cured. It gives meaty flavor to soups, braises, pasta sauces, and dishes of all kinds.

paprika, smoked sweet A Spanish specialty, smoked paprika is made from red chiles that have been smoked and then ground. It has a very earthy, smoky, and almost meaty flavor and a deep red color. Smoked paprika is available in sweet or mild (dulce), bittersweet (agridulce), and hot (picante) varieties.

parsnips These ivory-colored root vegetables, available in the fall and winter, closely resemble their carrot cousins. Parsnips have a slightly sweet, peppery flavor and a tough, starchy texture that softens with cooking.

peas Fresh peas of any variety add color and sweetness to a dish.

English English peas, or green peas as they are sometimes called, must be shelled before cooking. The shelled peas should be firm, bright green, and sweet enough to eat out of hand. Because their sugars quickly convert to starch, it is important to use English peas as soon as possible.

snow These flat green peas are eaten whole, pod and all. They have a crisp texture and fresh, green flavor with a mild sweetness. They can be used raw or cooked.

sugar snap Sugar snap peas look like plump snow peas, and like snow peas, they are eaten whole. They have a very crisp texture and sugary sweet flavor.

potatoes Different varieties of potatoes have different starch levels, making some a better match for certain cooking methods than others. The following are the varieties called for in this book.

fingerling Certain varieties of potatoes are called fingerlings because of their narrow, knobby shape. They are waxy, low-starch potatoes ideal for steaming or boiling.

new An immature potato that is low in starch, new potatoes are small in size and have very thin skins. They are available in spring and early summer.

red Round in shape, red potatoes have thin skins and a waxy texture. They are well-suited to roasting, boiling, and steaming.

russet Also called baking potato or Idaho potato, this variety is large in size with a rough brown skin. Its high starch content means that it cooks up dry and fluffy, making it perfect for frying, mashing, or baking.

yukon gold A medium-starch potato with thin skins and yellow flesh, Yukon gold potatoes have a sweet, buttery flavor. They are a good all-purpose potato.

radicchio A red-leafed chicory, radicchio has a bitter flavor and a tender but firm texture. *Radicchio di Verona* and *radicchio di Treviso* are the two common varieties; the former is globe shaped and the latter is narrow and tapered like Belgian endive. Radicchio can be cooked or used raw as a salad green.

red curry paste This Thai flavor base for spicy red curry is a complex blend of chiles, shallots, garlic, herbs, and spices. It is sold in small jars in well-stocked grocery stores and southeast Asian markets.

saffron The stigma of a small crocus which must be hand-picked and then dried, it takes several thousand flowers to yield just 1 ounce of dried saffron threads, explaining saffron's status as the most expensive spice. Luckily, a little goes a long way; just a pinch is needed to season foods with saffron's distinctive earthy flavor and lend a golden yellow hue.

salt, sea Sea salt is created by natural evaporation and contains no additives, so its flavor is crisp, with hints of mineral.

shallot Small members of the onion family, shallots have brownish skins and white flesh tinged with purple. Their flavor is a cross between sweet onion and garlic, and they are often used in recipes that would be overpowered by the stronger taste of onions.

soy sauce, dark A mixture of soybeans, wheat, and water is fermented to make this savory, salty sauce that is a common Asian ingredient and condiment. Dark soy sauce, used in Chinese cooking, is less salty than regular soy and is also thicker, darker, and sweeter due to the addition of molasses.

sriracha sauce The bright red-orange sauce is a mixture of ground chiles, tomatoes, vinegar, garlic, salt, and sugar. Originating in southern Thailand, this general-purpose sauce is used sparingly to add zest to a wide range of cooked dishes. It is also used a table condiment for many Southeast Asian dishes.

swiss chard These large, green, crinkled leaves have fleshy, ribbed stems. There are two main varieities: one with red stems and another with pearly white stems. Red-stemmed chard, also called rhubarb or ruby chard, has a slightly earthier flavor, while chard with white stems tends to be sweeter.

tomatoes These sweet-tart fruits are best in the summer at local farmstands and farmers' markets.

cherry These small, round tomatoes, usually about 1 inch in diameter, have quite thick skins and a full, sweet flavor. Red or yellow cherry tomatoes are the most common.

heirloom This term refers to tomato varieties that have been grown from select seeds that have never been hybridized. They come in a vast array of shapes, sizes, and colors, from large green fruits with stripes to small burgundy-black ones.

yellow pear These small pear-shaped tomatoes are low in acidity, which allows their sweetness to come to the fore.

vinegars Each type of vinegar has a unique flavor profile that makes it particularly suited to certain uses.

balsamic A specialty of the Italian region of Emilia-Romagna, primarily the town of Modena, balsamic vinegar is an aged vinegar made from the unfermented grape juice, or must, of white Trebbiano grapes. Aged in a series of wooden casks of decreasing sizes, each of a different wood, balsamic grows sweeter and more mellow with time. Long-aged balsamic vinegar is syrupy, intense, and intended to be used in small quantities as a condiment.

cabernet This specialty vinegar is a red wine vinegar that has been made by fermenting Cabernet Sauvignon wine for a second time. It has a bold acidity, but full, round flavor.

sherry True sherry vinegar from Spain, labeled *vinagre de Jerez*, has a slightly sweet, nutty taste, a result of aging in oak. It is especially good in salad dressings.

rice Commonly used in Chinese and Japanese cooking, rice vinegar is a clear, mild vinegar with a natural sweetness. Don't use seasoned rice vinegar in in place of plain rice vinegar.

wasabi A Japanese root similar but unrelated to horseradish, wasabi has a sharp, searing heat and a distinctive green color. Fresh wasabi is difficult to find, but It is commonly available as a powder or paste in well-stocked grocery stores and Japanese markets.

yogurt, Greek-style This plain yogurt, made in the style of traditional Greek yogurt, has a very thick, creamy texture and a rich, tangy flavor.

index

OXMOOR HOUSE

Oxmoor House books are distributed by Sunset Books
80 Willow Road, Menlo Park, CA 94025
Telephone: 650 324 1532
VP and Associate Publisher Jim Childs
Director of Marketing Sydney Webber
Oxmoor House and Sunset Books are divisions
of Southern Progress Corporation

WILLIAMS-SONOMA, INC.
Founder & Vice-Chairman Chuck Williams

WILLIAMS-SONOMA NEW FLAVORS SERIES
Conceived and produced by Weldon Owen Inc.
415 Jackson Street, Suite 200, San Francisco, CA 94111
Telephone: 415 291 0100 Fax: 415 291 8841
www.weldonowen.com

In Collaboration with Williams-Sonoma, Inc.
3250 Van Ness Avenue, San Francisco, CA 94109

A WELDON OWEN PRODUCTION
Copyright © 2008 Weldon Owen Inc. and Williams-Sonoma, Inc.
All rights reserved, including the right of reproduction
in whole or in part in any form.

First printed in 2008
Printed in Singapore

10 9 8 7 6 5 4 3 2 1
Library of Congress Cataloging-in-Publication Data is available.

ISBN-13: 978-0-8487-3256-1
ISBN-10: 0-8487-3256-1

This book is printed with paper harvested from well-managed forests
utilizing sustainable and environmentally sound practices.

WELDON OWEN INC.

Executive Chairman, Weldon Owen Group John Owen
CEO and President, Weldon Owen Inc. Terry Newell
Senior VP, International Sales Stuart Laurence
VP, Sales and New Business Development Amy Kaneko
Director of Finance Mark Perrigo

VP and Publisher Hannah Rahill
Executive Editor Jennifer Newens
Senior Editor Dawn Yanagihara
Associate Editor Julia Humes

VP and Creative Director Gaye Allen
Art Director Kara Church
Senior Designer Ashley Martinez
Designer Stephanie Tang
Photo Manager Meghan Hildebrand

Production Director Chris Hemesath
Production Manager Michelle Duggan
Color Manager Teri Bell

Photographer Kate Sears
Food Stylist Alison Attenborough
Prop Stylist Leigh Noe

Additional Photography Tucker+Hossler: Cover, pages 17, 21, 32, 33, 38, 49,
51, 56, 62, 65, 68, 70, 73, 77, 81, 82, 85, 89, 91, 93, 94, 97, 98, 113, 114, 117,
119, 120, 125, 129, 131, 133, 134, 137, 141, 149; Getty Images: altrendo
images, pages 14–15; Shutterstock: Dennis Debono, page 27; Simone van don
Berg, page 74; George P. Choma, pages 78–79; Dallas Events Inc., page 116;
Jupiter Images: Ronald Rammelkamp, pages 46–47; Heather Weston, page 58;
Polka Dot Images, pages 110–111.

ACKNOWLEDGMENTS

Weldon Owen wishes to thank the following individuals for their kind
assistance: Cover Food Stylist Erin Quon; Photo Assistants Victoria Wall and
Brittany Powell; Food Stylist Assistant Lillian Kang; Copy editor Judith Dunham;
Proofreaders Kathryn Shedrick and Carrie Bradley; Indexer Ken DellaPenta